A CABIN
IN THE
FOREST

A CABIN
IN THE
FOREST

HOW TO FIND, RENOVATE, AND RUN
THE PERFECT OFF-GRID RETREAT

ROXYANN SPANFELNER

Skyhorse Publishing

Skyhorse Publishing books may be purchased in bulk at special discounts for sales promotion, corporate gifts, fund-raising, or educational purposes. Special editions can also be created to specifications. For details, contact the Special Sales Department, Skyhorse Publishing, 307 West 36th Street, 11th Floor, New York, NY 10018 or info@skyhorsepublishing.com.

Skyhorse® and Skyhorse Publishing® are registered trademarks of Skyhorse Publishing, Inc.®, a Delaware corporation.

Visit our website at www.skyhorsepublishing.com.

10 9 8 7 6 5 4 3 2 1

Library of Congress Cataloging-in-Publication Data is available on file.

Cover design by Kai Texel
Cover photo credit: Getty Images

Print ISBN: 978-1-5107-6876-5
Ebook ISBN: 978-1-5107-7187-1

Printed in China

TABLE OF CONTENTS

Introduction

So much of what each of us does in our lives is a product of Divine Providence. I've seen it played out throughout my life. It is as though I'm traveling down a path dotted with ground-level lights placed on both sides that illuminate my way along it. If I take the wrong fork, the lights disappear and nothing seems to go right. But when I get back in the groove, everything falls into place again. Do you know what I mean? I think you do.

However, one may not see that so clearly when one is in the moment. It's only when you look back and reflect on the course you charted that everything suddenly makes sense. Such is the case with acquiring our cabin in the forest. As you will read in the opening chapter, I never really thought of owning a cabin. Little did I know that it had been a lifelong dream of my husband, Gary. Then an opportunity arose that made his dream obtainable.

And I went along for the ride, just as I did when we built our off-grid home twelve years ago—and what a ride that was. But that was a different (though awesome) adventure, a different experience, and a different book. Because as you will discover first-hand, having a cabin in the forest, or a cabin anywhere, is an entirely new experience. It is like nothing else that you could imagine.

It is my hope that this book captures your imagination. When you read what we did, why we did it, and more important, how we did it, you will realize you can do it too. The book makes it easy to see tangible ways you can achieve what we have, which we have outlined with many options and examples that you can modify to fit your own scenario.

1. Is It Time to Find a Cabin and Make It Your Own?

With this book, I hope I can help you on your journey to finding and shaping your own cabin retreat. First, however, I have to tell you that it is false to say we bought our fixer-upper cabin with the idea of it being a "Bug-Out Prepper Place," in lieu of a stay-at-home bunker choice. The reason? Gary, my husband (unbeknownst to me), had long dreamt of such a "get-away" simply for relaxation. Many feel the same. Now that all is said and done, as I look back over the bug-out research gumbo I exhumed to write my next book, *The Prepper's Bible*, I view our rustic retreat from both angles.

Why is a cabin such an alluring prepper option? Because it embraces the best of both worlds, offering a home away from home and if need-be a "safe-house insurance policy." Other not so immediate benefits include the fact that you will always have the option of selling it down the road and, in all probability, make a nice profit; or, if you never cash it in, you can pass it on as a legacy to children and grandchildren.

Five Reasonable Ways to Redefine the "Bug-Out" Labels That Just Make Sense

And while I say it in *The Prepper's Bible,* the following paragraphs are worth repeating. One can find innumerable bug-out expressions to add to the bug-out/prepper labels of today. Some have been around for eons. Here are a few to review: From the whimsical "Born To Be Free," "Getting Back To Nature," and Ted Nugent's more recent "Spirit Of The Wild," to the more ominous "Doomsday Preppers" and "Survivalists" terminology of today. These two latter labels denote a sharp escalation away from the former bug-out "pattern" in the sense of urgency they engender; almost a frenzied scramble toward an alternative lifestyle. But if you ask me, it's a rewire to the correct way to live, or let's say the way we were *meant* to live.

While these few labels are so familiar and evocative, they are also extremely indicative of what we as a society are yearning to rediscover. Beyond the slang, it boils down to five basics that I put in my bug-out prepper book and double down on here:

▶ The original cabin in the forest.

1. Inner Peace (*That old eyeball roller phrase*): While the Doomsday Sayers may be prepping for biblical apocalyptic tribulations and disasters, there remains not a thing you can do about the final battle at Armageddon; and no one, though some tried, can predict when that might happen. The end times that the world's been perpetually in—forecast now for ages— has caused much needless unrest. But one can find peace if one is able to focus on the ways to achieve it. And they are all free.

2. Quiet Time Alone (*To think straight*). How many of us have five minutes right now to gather thoughts, to get more organized, to set up a "to-do" list or even a bucket-list for future dreams and goals? Just do it. It's satisfying and freeing.

3. The Sweetness of Simplicity. This means literally simplifying our lifestyle or, better yet, just finding ways to appreciate it by first stripping away the materialistic me-isms and determining what is really important, like family together time or time spent with a sick friend. Or though trite, how about just appreciating the Earth's beauty? When my mom lay dying in hospital, she looked at me and said: "People don't appreciate the beauty of our Earth anymore." That hit me hard. Since then, I thank God for it every day.

4. Spirituality and Grasping Peace of Mind. What is really vital in this life is getting in touch with the *next one*. Establish a pathway to it even if you carve only five minutes a day to do so in prayer, in word, in deed, or in all three. It has instant upbeat effects: You'll feel literally uplifted about yourself, others, and your surroundings when you do. Try. It works.

◀ Fully restored cabin in the forest.

▶ Here, Greta is getting a sip of cold spring water from our perpetual fountain. We rarely turn it off, though we do have a valve to control the height of the water. It is fed directly from the spring through an underground pipe from our tank storage.

▶ Freshly painted log barrier to prevent vehicles from going over the steep hillside. Gary cut the dying trees and placed them here with his tractor and chain lift.

5. Find Your "Frame" with Plain and Simple R&R=R. If you learn to rest and relax, you will rejuvenate. Whether an hour with a good book, a power nap, or best of all a jaunt to your cabin hideout, the key is then in hand to open all four of the above doors. The tail chasing stops, you're prepped to the nines, and life is finally in order: in short, you've gathered all your own destiny's possibilities around you in a perfect frame, and maximized your full potential.

Prepare for the Double Duty Day (Make Your Cash Outlay Work Overtime)

Who doesn't want a little R & R to rejuvenate? But just holding down a job to preserve a normal lifestyle's needs—paying a mortgage, saving for kids' college, finding affordable health insurance—is hard to do without throwing a retreat into the mix as a safe-haven and a means to relax. Who can afford that? But my question is: Can you afford not to?

When expending, find solace knowing that if a cabin can do double duty during a short crisis or a long-term meltdown shelter, the dividend on the cash outlay grows exponentially. But meantime, use it as a fun spot to unzip from life's stresses and just enjoy. In the coming chapters, you'll learn the top ten list of must haves in choosing a cabin retreat. After that, I'll detail how we concentrated on the basics of survival: food, a heating and cooking source, shelter, water, and power, and how we, in the end, achieved inner peace.

2. The Reasons Why We Bought Our Cabin

Our decision to get a cabin meant we had to temporarily amend our R&R calculation. After all, a rustic retreat that is in some level of disrepair does not equal immediate Rest and Relaxation (at least not instantly). This is when the rose-colored specs fall off and you are faced with three options once you buy:

1. Leave it alone and wear extremely obscured rose-colored glasses forever.
2. Patch and fix it for the rest of our lives, making us slaves to maintenance.
3. Strip her down to the rafters for a complete redo and no future worries.

We chose option No. 3 without hesitation. Both my husband Gary and I are no strangers to the rolling-up-of-shirt-sleeves, dirty, hands-on kind of hard work. Later, we'd find that we enjoyed the R&R part of our retreat even more as we recalled our toils and savored the outcome from them. Gary also enjoys challenges and has a sense of vision I do not share. Heck, that's what lead us to build our off-grid primary home, but that's another book. And honestly, while I saw the great beauty of our surroundings, I mainly saw the work and effort it would take to get our cabin into usable shape. Even the logistics to get a crew and the supplies we'd need cabin-side was more than I could fathom. Gratefully, I can always put my trust in my husband who, after thirty years of marriage, has intuitively put us on all the right paths. We've scored big time as a result, meaning we've enjoyed some truly life-changing adventures.

▶ The lower cabin before renovations.

◄ The lower cabin after renovations.

◄ Front view of lower cabin. Gary, with help from Steve Downey, moved the very heavy entire front deck from our upper cabin down the hill and placed it here. Gary then rebuilt the back deck, shored up all the roofing, and patched the existing tin roof.

Here's what he saw as the ten must-haves for getting a cabin; these are what sold him on the dwelling we eventually settled on:

1. **Abundant Water.** I don't care where it is; if you choose a cabin, it must have a good water source. My husband always says, "Buying land is the best investment out there—so long as it has water, because water is life." The cabin we chose is almost at the top of a mountain, at the headwaters of a beautiful creek with year-round waterfalls and extremely active spring area within. These springs (gravity flow) appealed immensely to Gary, though the cabin itself, the property around it, and the road into it were in grave disrepair. The plentiful water, in his eyes, added immense value.

The bottom line: Don't buy property without water of some kind. You do not want to haul water, as Gary's cousin needs to do at his home in Fairbanks, Alaska, or a neighbor in the area where we've built our primary home. Obviously, it is a hassle to haul water, no matter if you need it for vacations or when you really need it for an emergency. You want water on hand to drink freely, wash yourself and your clothes, cook, clean dishes, and for plumbing purposes. Those are only a few creature comforts afforded through water that make it both indispensible for life and, consequently, make life worth living.

The Miracle of Gravity Flow Water. While an antiquated gravity-flow system and tank system were in place (with a line also to a perpetually flowing fountain almost at the cabin's door) from the spring above the cabin, many changes were needed, beginning with clearing a wildly over-grown footpath to the spring. Gary also installed a much-needed new 3000-gallon tank, plus a filtration system that allows for clean, silt-free water to the cabin. And before we could do that, we had to do a lot of trenching and add new PVC lines (to replace the existing rotted-out aluminum pipe) to connect it from the spring, into the tank, and then on down to the cabin. Afterward, I'd be able to turn on the water without power, and the miracle

of gravity-flow, abundant, "self-pressurized" water for cooking, washing, and bathing now gushes out fresh and clean.

In addition, Gary had an overflow plan to handle the tank's overflow from the spring that was diverted in a separate line away from the cabin's water line. Though I detail this below, he had dug this line down the steep hillside from tank to cabin with a hand trencher, and then continued with the diversion line beyond—laying PVC pipe all the way—so that the fresh-water overflow would spill out unwasted into a small, freshly dug-out trout pond that he put in place after the fire-hazard of trees and dense brush around the cabin had been cleared.

2. **Location.** The location of our second home was ideally situated not excessively far from our primary home, at an elevation between four thousand to five thousand feet. Having a location that is not more than an hour or so distant from your home and attainable in an emergency away from high traffic areas is a huge plus when buying a retreat. But with gigantic maple and oak trees, pines, Douglass firs, and massive maple and oaks—to name just some of the flora covering the vistas—it was vastly different from the eight-hundred-foot elevation on our valley ranch of rolling oak-covered hillsides. And though we have some huge oak trees on the ranch, the mountain oaks and other trees take one's breath away with their sheer depth and breadth.

The steep, beautiful US Forest Service mountainsides surrounding us were all to our liking, uninhabited except for bears and deer, allowing for virtually no walk-in visits (unless by the unbelievable adventurous and in shape). This would include my husband, who clambered all over the treacherous shale-covered mountains above us. He even hiked—if one calls scaling vertical terrain "hiking"—to the peak where his unexpected arrival totally surprised the summer fire look-out person stationed at the remote tower. (So much for being "*alone* in the wilderness.")

Speaking of having to expect the unexpected, we installed several trail cameras around our cabin and also on the roadway leading up to it. These now contain photographs a few two-legged trespassers, plus four-legged ones such as bears, deer, as well as mountain lions. Yes, it is rugged country, in all ways.

The snow really comes in winter at that elevation, laying down a thick white blanket, freezing the landscape with a brushstroke making its silent beauty heart stopping. Still, even then the county roadway is accessible—and somewhat maintained—enabling us to reach the cabin almost year-round to enjoy even this season. (Important for everyone to note: you'll need year-round accessibility to your retreat, since it is never known when disaster's hammer will bang down on the nail!) But then the snow melts and spring breaks, bringing brilliant wildflowers over the slopes; and summer, while at times hot, has lovely mountain breezes and sapphire skies so intense that your eyes water when you look up. When fall comes sneaking, the smells and changing colors make me think of pumpkin pie and turkey dinners. Each season holds a glorious beauty to relax in and enjoy.

3. **Neighbors.** For the most part we are blessed by our few and far between neighbors, and as a dear ranching friend once said to us, "good fences make good neighbors." In that terrain, the countryside itself builds a lush fence. All around above us is US Forest Service, a private logging company, and that handful of neighbors who'd go out of their way to help you if they are there. Many of those people on the mountain, as it has been referred to, have kept the property in their families for generations. Gary already knew and respected most of them. Those he didn't know, he made it his business to quickly meet. And yes, while you want your privacy at such a location, it is also critical to know the lay of the land and everyone on it and around you. Most important, you want to be a good neighbor—and at the same time a neighbor who sets boundaries. In other words, you respect them and they'll respect you.

4. **Almost Year-Round Access Could Easily Be Made Year-Round.** The almost year-round accessibility can be quickly made year-round with a few pieces of equipment. One such piece of equipment used to do so is the county-owned road grader, whose services provide, well, road grading. Some other friends my husband soon made included the country office roads' official and the road crews themselves, who can be invaluable. You'd be surprised how far a simple *thank you!* phone call can take you. Another great little tool is a snowmobile, if you're in for some adventure (be sure to train with them first), and don't forget the aforementioned useful four-wheel-drive auto. However, snowmelt at our location is usually quick and not too deep to navigate through.

5. **The First Survival Basic: Food—Your Stockpile and Mother Nature's.** Though we are remote, not only is our stockpile easily accessible with a conventional vehicle, or even our EMP-proof (Electromagnetic Pulse) 1951 Willy's Jeep if need be, it is also well stocked. By this I'm referring to first-aid supplies, canned food, dry goods (much stored in five-gallon buckets and seal-proof screw-down lids, now at Tractor Supply stores), and running water. All are must-haves—along with chocolate chips. But we also have access to food from nature, including wild game such as deer, fowl, and fish; all of which abound on our 80-acre property. And though the cabin had a few lovely old apple and apricot trees, we balanced them with twenty more fruit trees. If only deer and bear had studied the unspoken rules of etiquette and left well enough alone!

6. **Historical Value.** While not a necessity, if you find property of historical value, it is a bonus. This property was of historical value and the home of geological formations on which 1950s studies were based, but that was just a tip of the rocky, shale-iced cake. By that I mean that although finding a getaway with historical value wasn't initially on our top-ten list, the saga behind our old cabin and other all but falling-down buildings (such as the little shower house, the overshot-wheel cabin, and the original 1913 Timber Claim Cabin) on the property enriched our personal experience—especially during the grimy, hard-toiling period of renovation. That was just our lucky reward. The land

still boasts much of the landmark logging flume, part of a turn-of-the-century logging camp, and a host of logging roads crisscrossing the property. Some were unusable, but Gary restored them so it that we now have complete access to our property.

The tiny 1913 lower cabin, so called because it sits below our cabin, had all but given up the ghost and was full to overflowing with one hundred years' accrual of castoffs. But somehow, wading past the animal droppings and discarded paraphernalia, Gary found a reward: A pencil-scribed message atop the door lintel, *"Timber Claim Cabin, built in 1913 for $400."* It appeared to be signed, but regrettably the signature was illegible. Still, this thumbprint gave us an uplifting vision of what had transpired here. We later learned that a woman had been hired to cook there for the crew—by

▲ A vintage flat iron the woman in the cabin, and I'm guessing my grandmother too, had probably used—the epitome of manual labor. (And we think modern irons are hard work!)

▲ Inside of the lower cabin.

woodstove, of course. We even found her little old wooden ironing board amidst the rubble, 'signed' with singe marks and stapled canvas remnants. Priceless! We've situated it against a wall. Personally, I thought, what was *she* thinking? Then I recalled that back then everyone ironed everything except perhaps socks, and with fire-heated irons. I know because my own grandmother had told me about this. Here is an example of the type of iron she used:

7. **A Haven of Peace.** As I've mentioned, "Inner Peace" isn't so corny. Not only should it be vital to find a safe haven in your retreat, but also critical is a peace of mind refuge. While my mom said she truly enjoyed ironing, and said pressing items into flat-crisp submission gave her a sense of peace, an iron at the cabin was not my way of attaining inner peace. So yes, it had to be a safe haven and more. I am a firm believer that such a place is actually not only good for the body and mind, but it also enriches the soul if located in the right setting.

8. **A Place to Recharge Your Batteries.** Gary had called the ranch where we ultimately built our off-grid home the place he always went to recharge his batteries. Now with new majestic cabin vistas to value and admire, he'd ramped his battery pack up for a high-voltage, off-the-charts charge. What accomplishes such a charge? It was in the region's sense of immortality. I call it "The Land That Time Forgot". It was the huge trees, the terrain, and the boundless water—complete with thunder-ing waterfalls that could be heard a mile away as we walked along our logging roads down to them. It was all magical. But magic holds singular

meaning for each of us. My dear ninety-two-year-old German friend, Dorie (I spoke of her in my other books), and I call it *Märchen*. It means fairy tale in German. Find your *personal* fairy-tale spot.

9. **The Sense of Trusted Community.** You need trusted community around you at your tiny retreat—just as in your daily residence. They should be like-minded independents who take care of and think for themselves when the chips are down. But, at the same time, if need be, they can band together with a communal self-interest.

10. **The Ever-Practical Financial: A Good Investment.** Is land ever a bad investment? No, almost never. Even unimproved, remote, cabin-less real estate is a great asset and will quickly increase in value. Why? Because it is in demand for all the reasons I've laid out above. Not a place to literally *escape* to, but more to get back to the fundamentals of living and appreciation of the simple joys found therein. If you can find a turn-key place, or a way to innovatively make it your own, you can all but name your selling price in future.

I'll give you an example of this as far as a bug-out place is concerned: The Reagan Ranch. President Ronald Reagan had his own 688-acre Santa Barbara bug-out bungalow retreat long before bug out was a twinkle-term in some writer's eye. It is called Rancho del Cielo (Sky Ranch) on a cliffside overlooking the ocean, bought in 1974, as he was finishing up his second term as California's governor. If you've ever seen, read, or heard about this ranch, you'll know what I mean.

It was to be his refuge as he made his 1976 and 1980 presidential bids. The road leading up to it becomes a twisting one-laner. Coming and going, rounding each blind bend, you honk your horn to alert any on-coming traffic of your approach. The little bungalow itself is a study of eclectic cabinesque simplicity, not just tiny but simply furnished with no set style; pea-green vinyl on the shoe-box-size kitchen floor, twin beds in the guestroom with handmade quilts, and a shower so small you'd wonder how

Nancy fit in it, let alone Ronnie with this six-foot-plus frame. But he loved it. He also took every opportunity to go, inviting heads of state along—including the likes of Soviet leader Mikhail Gorbachev and The Queen of England. Preposterous! Didn't he care what they thought? Not a wit. Here's the beauty of his philosophy on the matter:

> *"From the first day we saw it, Rancho del Cielo cast a spell over us. No place before or since has ever given Nancy and me the joy and serenity it does."*

Gary and I know just what President Reagan meant. He found his *Märchen*. And the president's vital need to have his getaway exemplifies what I've written on these pages. But here it is quite simple again: It kept him grounded and in touch with all that is central in life. And when he took to the saddle, or drove around the ranch in his CJ6 Willy's Jeep (Mrs. Reagean bought it for him as a Christmas present in 1963), or cut wood and cleared brush, it brought balance to his life, clarity to his mind, and kept him in touch with America's roots.

Photo courtesy of The Reagan Library

▲ The President behind the wheel of his CJ6.

The President relished the chance to drive himself around the ranch. Originally utility green, the California National Guard painted the Jeep red with white pinstripes as a going-away present before the end of Reagan's two terms as governor. "He loved driving it," retired Secret Service agent John R. Barletta recalls.

"He did a lot with this Jeep. And I never remember it breaking down." (Note: This is just the type of vehicle that keeps going even after an EMP (Electromagnetic Pulse) may take down other vehicles.)

To summarize the "why it was a good investment" list: Like the Reagans, we are investing in ourselves, our future, and our peace of mind, and are not planning for financial gain or doubling our investment, as we have no intention of selling. And it's fine to call it a bug-out from life as we are living it; I'm okay with hearing that today. But now I hope you can see, as I do, what it really is: It is an escape into a reconnect to life, instead of a disconnect from it. President Reagan figured that out over forty years ago.

▲ Left: Rancho Del Cielo. At Right: The Reagans with Queen Elizabeth II and the Duke of Edinburgh, March 1, 1983. Note Reagan's smile of pride.

3. Time to Roll Up Our Sleeves and Attempt to Accomplish a Mission Impossible

Just like the President did on his Rancho, at times one just has to roll up their sleeves and get dirty—for a "mission impossible" to become a mission accomplished. And while our fairy-tale spot didn't have seven dwarfs, it did have a prince charming who works harder than one hundred dwarfs. He also has a magic all his own to make things click. I hired him (he works for food) on the spot. Of course, he was my own ever-lovin husband!

But due to the state of disrepair that the cabin and property had fallen into—in part because of the owner's age, an eighty-five-year-old widower who dearly loved it but could only dream of taking it in hand—we came to some raw-wound conclusions. Just to bring it back to a livable condition and make it the low upkeep retreat we desired (mainly for easy care in *our* old age), it would need not only added cash outlay but also mainly a huge dedicated investment of hard physical work. Once an adjusted lower price was agreed upon—which factored in revisions for disrepair—escrow closed fast and it was time to get to work. Summer was waning and we had to make hay before snow fell.

Cabin Perimeter Cleanup

The work began with the cabin's perimeter cleanup; a huge undertaking in itself, as so many large and dead trees surrounded and endangered the cabin. Gary trailered his tractor, bucket, and brush-rake (which saves us untold man-hours at our home as well), pulling it behind his truck in the predawn hours to avoid overheating as he climbed on the twisting road. With the tractor then on site, it was time to clear the thicket of trees, brush, stumps, and berries all but encapsulating the cabin belt. It was vital as fire defense and to open the heretofore utterly hidden million-dollar view to the valley floor forty miles below. To help in this mammoth endeavor, Gary hired a three-man crew with chainsaws and a chipper. He toiled alongside them, and hauled away with his tractor what could not be chipped or cut up for firewood. After two twelve-hour days, much of the crucial cleanup was complete—including felling and removing of three huge dying trees near the cabin, a must for safety.

▼ Front of the shower house. Notice the pipe on the upper right, below the deer horns. The is where the water was piped in for showering.

▲ Dead and dying trees were removed from the area around the cabin. For safety, they were taken down in sections. In the photo above right, the stump is being cut away in sections so that, eventually, the deck would fit over it.

▲ To eliminate the need to burn brush later, and to create a perimeter around the cabin to aid in fire protection, the tree trimmers used a chipper on much of the brush from the trees.

▲ Some examples of the heavy growth around the cabin before we went to work. A huge thicket of berry bushes had overrun the entire length of the back perimeter.

Once the rotted deck was removed and demolished, the cabin renovation could begin.

In addition, a massive overgrowth of berry patches needed ousting. And while blackberries are delish in pies or jams, the bushes all around our "yard" were producing not only luscious fruit, but also fat, juicy timber rattlers. I didn't know the rattlers near our cabin were green, like the forest, until Gary kindly showed me. Mother Nature had designed them to blend in with their surroundings!

So how was I to thwart Mother Nature's perfect balance? I made it my job—in addition to making berry pies—to take up raking: raking deep layers of pine needles, leaf duff, and pine cones into piles for burning, and last but not least boulders and rubble. I raked for weeks, even in my sleep, all around the boundary.

For fire control? Yes! But I also strove to pare our border down to a non-green dirt carpet for ease of snake detection and removal, well before Gary, Greta, or I might step on one. Then, just as Peter Graves' *Mission Impossible* message self-destructs in a smoky cloud (once his mission was gleaned); that very winter, my piles went up in smoke too. Mission accomplished!

Road Cleanup

The next step was broadening our cleanup efforts and making the several miles of road into the property and the long-abandoned and rock-covered logging roads all over the acreage more accessible. We also had to remove branches and trees, fill potholes, and widen the narrow track, both on the ground and overhead. To do this Gary brought in a dozer and grader and used his chainsaw and a power-pole saw for overhanging tree branch removal. It made an immense transformation. Before this, the lack of visibility and narrowness to the vertical fall-off side of the roadway, chiefly in muddy and icy conditions, meant certain death if one slid over the bank. In fact, Gary has worked on it even more since, using his four-wheel-drive tractor with its invaluable box scraper float hooked behind. In addition, as a Father's Day gift last year, I hired three tree trimmers to help him *really* clear back the road of encroaching Manzanita and more dead or dying trees (which he piled again on his tractor's brush rake and hauled off). In the future these needs are now minimal.

MUCKING OUT THE CABIN'S INTERIOR.

Finally it was time to turn our hand to the cabin's sadly neglected interior. Rat and mouse evidence was all over inside: Inside the furniture, acorn shells were stashed under sofa cushions, in the oven insulation, in the contents of dresser drawers—all were ruined from droppings and urine, as were the dishes and kitchen countertops. Plus there were dropping all over the vinyl flooring. Frankly I didn't know where to start. Ultimately, the mucking out grew into three piles:

1. Garbage: This went into huge heavy-duty contractor bags (I stopped counting at twenty), which we had to cart home and throw out there. Most of these things had been destroyed by the rat infestation.

2. Goodwill items: These things could be cleaned up and sent to a new home— including the two sofas in the living room. I painstakingly cleaned and wrapped them in tarps for the trip down the mountain in our trailer. They eventually found good homes! Two sofas would not fit into our new, almost wall-less floor plan (although three vintage recliners donated by friends work great), as we needed to remove old windows, replace them, and then add sliding doors in the tiny living room to a new walkout viewing deck.

3. Keepers: Things that appealed to us and could be repaired or were of historical value that would go back in cabin after the renovation.

▶ Mucking out the kitchen and trying not to feel overwhelmed. This is where we developed the "three pile rule."

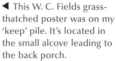

◀ This W. C. Fields grass-thatched poster was on my 'keep' pile. It's located in the small alcove leading to the back porch.

Some of the few things we were able to salvage were the original 1920 propane-fueled Servel refrigerator, and a 1950 O'Keefe & Merrit gas stove. For two days, I cleaned (degreased) the stove and then followed up the process with a vintage appliance repairman, Vern of Vern's Vintage Appliances. He agreed to make

◀ The Servel refrigerator was originally directly across from its current position.

the seventy-five-mile one-way ride (the odds *alone* of finding a repairer/restorer of these appliances is almost nil) up to our retreat, evaluate them, and then service them. The best news? He did so at a very reasonable price.

▶ An example of our new window, which is deeper and wider than the original. To the right is our reconditioned 1920 Servel propane refrigerator. We have to light the pilot light to turn it on.

Despite this, I didn't think I'd ever be able to cook on that stove—though its enameled-speckled blue interior now gleams—as it stunk to high heaven when he burner tested. While Vern declared it standard, saying it'd soon blow out, I begged to differ and said it smelled like rat urine. Ugh. Vern and Gary looked at each other and Vern suggested that they take the side panels off the stove to see if rodents had gotten through the internal insulation. Sure enough, on one side, rat-damaged insulation was found.

▲ The original kitchen countertops, made out of floor vinyl. (Yes, that is rat poop.) In the second photo, I'm holding the tacks that had been used to hold the vinyl to the wood.

Fortuitously, Vern said it was cosmetic. They'd not yet chewed the mechanics or wiring, which would have made the stove irredeemable. Now, a show of hands please: Who wants to remove all the smelly, discolored insulation? Vern put his hand up first. (God bless him!) Plus he ordered new insulation, which Gary installed.

Afterward, I stood by skeptically as he lit the burners—but lo and behold, the rank smell was gone! I'll be forever thankful for our fortitude over this bygone-era relic as providentially, my grandma lovingly taught me to cook and make bread on one just like it! But how does this one *actually* cook now? Amazing.

◀ Secondary view of original cabin, showing the screened porch that had to be removed because it had been added on to an already weak and rotting deck.

◀ This is what the screened porch area looks like today. Note the stairway that goess straight up to the deck and front door, rather than right-facing as before. Gary designed it this way for aesthetics and practical purposes.

We weren't so lucky with the woodstove that heated the cabin. It was old, cracked, and heavy. Incidentally, the fire-retardant wall behind the stove consisted of aluminum foil held up with more of those handy thumbtacks. And while I continued mucking out the cabin, Gary got to work on the old cellar below, then the shower house directly outside the cabin, plus the other two outlying buildings I've described. Over a century's worth of stockpiling needed assessing and disposal.

▶ Screened porch removal—not an easy task. All boards throughout the project that could be reused were saved.

▶ There goes the screen porch.

◄ Removal of the deck under the screened porch.

Our "least wanted list" included twenty or more old rat-eaten mattresses and rusted springs and just plain rotted-out boxes and debris. Literally little to no walk or step-around room was to be found. Gary paid his friend's teenage son to come up and load up all the scrap metal on his dad's huge equipment trailer and he also got to keep all the recycle cash, amounting to hundreds of dollars, that he'd accumulated. And of course he brought his girlfriend. But he failed to impress her over his meeting up with one of those timber rattlers when helping Gary heft sheet after sheet of tin (piled three feet high against the lower cabin) up hill to the flatbed trailer. He refused to go back down for fear of unearthing more, and Gary finished as he watched. Still, he made two more trips up to the cabin, hauling away huge and heavy trailer loads of metal/tin recyclables off the place.

◄ Examples of all the rot under the deck.

▶ Another example of rotted wood under the deck.

▶ Rotted timbers in this area under the deck were shored up with concrete blocks.

◀ In the lower cabin is a caboose stove, which we fire with coal and small pieces of wood.

◀ This handmade table was in the basement of the upper cabin. The cabinet above it came from the upper cabin's original kitchen (I painted it green). The windows are original.

▶ The original screen door, with new screening. The cot was salvaged and upgraded with a new mattress.

4. Finding the Right Contractor to Restructure the Cabin

During that month-long, muck-out-fest phase, we researched contractor availability and searched for one who was really qualified to reconstruct our cabin. It was a tall order. Finally, after traveling the distance to our remote hideaway, Steve Downey of Acorn Construction reviewed the situation and took the job. He was a perfect fit, and not because of his Acorn company name—he'd be surrounded by oak trees—but due to his experience. He was imminently qualified, as he understood the logistics and the need to make every trip count, as Home Depot was a long, bumpy one- and one-half-hour ride one way. Why was he so perfect? While he did commercial work as well (he'd just completed a bank renovation), he also had an annual winter contract with the National Park Service and worked on, among other things, their historical cabin renovations. The providential key here was he was now between jobs. He just finished the bank and wanted a little summer R&R himself, before his winter obligations kicked into high gear. At first hesitant due to logistics, once he'd seen the setting and knew our mission, Steve agreed to take us and the job on with only a couple of stipulations:

- If he could fit it into his schedule and if we weren't in a rush.
- If he would be allowed to come only one or two days a week with one hired man.

We were all in. After mapping out a four-part contract (below), we then settled on a start date. Steve also made a promise—as did my husband. He vowed when he and his crew arrived, they'd work long days. He kept his word, arriving at dawn with his one- or two-man (and sometimes his painter, Kirk, came too) crew depending on the need, and they worked hard ten-hour-plus days. (I know, since I was often there working on my own projects, like raking. Sometimes I'd alternate that with digging. I carved out the area behind the cabin for a retaining wall, which would be built later to stop water runoff (and ensuing rot) against the new back wall of the cabin.)

And what was my husband's promise? That he'd work right alongside Steve. And he did. Starting with the demolition, pier post installation, the tractor hauling away of debris to two gigantic piles for later burning (an invaluable labor and cost saver to the contractor as he then didn't need to stack it all or make countless trips to the town dump), and the repair of the two lower cabins.

The Four-Part Plan Mapped Out Between Our Contractor and Us

When building or renovating, have a detailed contract, with stipulations you as a cabin owner must have, along with a fitting completion-phase for each payment schedule. If you hammer this out first, your project and your relationship with your contractor will have a satisfying and harmonious outcome, devoid of costly surprises. Though like to our home's complex contract that had an added contract for alternative power (a ten-point plan for our building contractor and alternative contractor documented in my book, *How To Build A Perfect Off-Grid Home—Let The Sun Rain Down On Your Solar [Second Edition]*), our cabin pact clearly could be much simpler.

What's our key contract advice if you're restoring a cabin? Know as best as you can what you're getting into beforehand. Still, realize in fixer-upper rustic cabin land, it's illogical to have all "i's" dotted. After all, ours was to be a deep redo. But, you can make everything as black and white as possible. In addition, have some reserve cash and a contractor who will go the distance with you. Before each payment draw is made (through you or your bank), in case of problems be sure you have that phase completed so issues get resolved before the ink dries on the check. Our four phases included: I. the demo, reframing, and window placement; II. installing a metal roof and exterior siding, deck frame, exterior painting, and exterior doors; III. installing all plumbing and electrical, plus building the decks, railing, exterior stairs, and new interior stairs to a brand-new loft area that Gary planned; and IV. completion phase, including painting of the interior doors, walls, and ceiling, the laying of flooring, and the repair of lower cabins. At project's end, before the final payment, do a walk-through together to ensure all is in order.

Phase I. DEMO, REFRAMING, AND WINDOW PLACEMENT

When you decide on a deep redo, you need to look at the bright side of things. And that is: After the partial demo, it's much easier to move (and/or eliminate) windows and doors and make them bigger or smaller. And in Phase I of our project, we did just that. We swapped a living room window with a sliding door that would open to a new, repositioned deck placed so we could fully enjoy the complete valley view (revealed after tree and brush elimination) sixty miles distant. Phase I embraced all exterior demo, including the rotted east and south decks, completion of new deck foundation work (footings poured and joisting finished), the one-inch walls on the original part of the cabin changed to 2x4 formation, and placement of all new windows except for the bubble-glass hatch one in the bathroom.

◀ A large stockpile of items that needed to go "downtown."

▶ The basement before the clean-out. A daunting task, to say the least.

▶ After the clean-up. Middle and bottom photos show an organized, clean basement. Note the collection of vintage saws hanging on the wall.

◀ The lower cabin was literally filled to the rafters with debris and bed springs.

◀ Dustin Mason and his girlfriend loading his trailer with metal to go to the recycler's.

Before the footings for the deck could be poured, the holes needed to be dug in the concrete-hard earth. It was bone-jarring work, but vital to hold up the heavy surrounding deck and 2x6 supports that Gary had stipulated for added strength.

First, however, he aided in demo-ing of a screen porch that had been built in the seventies on top of the (even then) obviously weak and rotted deck structural base (and the pile of rotten mattresses inside). All was removed and both the deck and stairway were repositioned. Then, after hand picking with Steve and storing reusable timbers and wood, Gary's countless tractor trips of hauling rotten boards and burnable debris away began.

▶ Getting things stripped away. Here's Steve's hired man, Milton, checking the original cedar siding. We kept all lower cedar from the floor level down. The upper portion was replaced.

▶ Steve with Milton, right, laying the loft flooring.

At that time, in order to stop future water and rot damage from runoff down the steep hillside behind the cabin, we planned on installing a retaining wall. Gary had already chipped the invasive wisteria vine roots out from the concrete "dirt" (we'd removed a rickety arbor and the mostly dead vines earlier) located there. This is when I dropped my rake and picked up a shovel to "dig," and squared up the rock-hard earth to lay the groundwork for the wall's concrete blocks. It was a very hot summer day but luckily Gary's total focus was inside working on the appliances with Vern (who'd driven two and a half hours to our cabin), so he was oblivious of my work until I was done—a good thing, as he wouldn't have wanted me to do it alone. But I got the job done, as did Gary and Vern.

◄ More loft work. Check out the view!

◄ The rebuilding of the walls of the original portion of the cabin built in 1920. It originally was one-inch board by four-inch "bat," with no two-by-four reinforcements. The walls were one inch thick, with newspaper filling all of the cracks. This area was the bedroom.

Phase II. METAL ROOF/CABIN SIDING/DECK FRAME/EXTERIOR PAINTING

With Phase I done, and the clutter and debris gone, we could clearly visualize from the skeleton frame the new look of our tiny abode. But we were still careful to retain the cabin's historical value and basic structure too, including its original stalwart hand-hewn solid log foundation. We were also able to preserve the smaller cabins and their rustic character.

Straightaway we began Phase II, adding meat to the bones by first removing the old corrugated tin roof, which leaked and was rusted and rolled back in places, then installing a new metal roof.

At this point we also took the opportunity to extend the roof with a small overhang above the front-door deck area, as it got really hot when the summer sun beat directly down. Now shielded, it's a cool summer afternoon reading spot, as breezes often blow across it. We relax

and lounge there—even Greta carries her own bed out for naps, alternated by trips downstairs to revel on the cool green lawn we planted. Her rolling, rooting, and groaning in deep contentment exhibits to us the true, simple essence of rest and relaxation.

As the metal roof went on, it seemed like a real shelter. The two replacement exterior doors and the new one for the tiny loft, plus the weatherproof concrete board siding put up where needed and which matched to the existing heavy, wide-board cedar siding, completed the now tightly sealed sanctuary. Then the entire cabin's exterior, the repaired shower house, lower cabin, and overshot Pelton wheel cabin were treated to a coat of thick, dark-chocolate-colored paint. In this phase, the much-awaited new loft area was internally also rough-framed: This room was born when the cabin's steep roofline was revealed during the partial demo—laid bare after

▶ The old tin coming off.

◄ A sampling of the wood and other supplies needed for remodeling.

◄ Total rebuild of the back porch that was caving in.

the layers of water-damaged low-hung seven-foot ceiling was peeled away. The new vertical space gave Gary an idea: he and Steve mapped out a small ten- by- fourteen-foot loft, which included a walkout to a tiny "lookout" set atop the lower deck, with little added cost.

▶ The finished back porch with a screen door on each end. The stairs are original.

▶ The whole bottom side of the original west-facing cabin. The rotten boards were cut away, and replaced with treated beams shored up and placed on concrete peer posts.

Phase III. DECK FLOORING AND RAILING/ PLUMBING AND ELECTRICAL

Now in Phase III, it was time to transform our new outdoor living space with a deck floor. What a huge change screwing down the deck boards and adding the railing made! Then Kirk came to stain the added outdoor living space. This deck embodied a renovated but attached north porch that had been collapsing from both ends. Mercifully, we were able to repurpose the existing stairs to this separate porch area—which we enclosed, adding two small windows to the two heavy metal screen doors (later bear-tested, with claw marks to prove it) on each end. This outdoor space can serve as an extra sleeping quarters; we could tell it had been used for this purpose in the past, due to the two iron beds found there with, yet again, piles of rotted mattresses in need of a good airing, which they promptly got— on their way to the dump. Then we vented and plumbed the back porch for a washer/dryer (if later desired) and installed the hot water heater. Yes, the joys of hot water; long, guilt-free, spring water–fed hot showers were almost in our grasp. Alas, the new shower stall installation was scheduled in phase four. But the efficient hot water heater was now connected—as was our 1920 propane *Servel* icebox and O'Keefe & Merritt stove—to a newly refurbished gas line and regulator attached to a new 500-gallon tank. Vern, the handy appliance aficionado, installed both. The key here: hire multi-tasking experts. It not only allowed us to check the appliances gas flow ahead of schedule, it saved us time, effort, and cash as the propane company didn't need to make an extra trip or two, first troubleshooting, then coming back with the right parts. So when feasible, hire contractors who cover multiple bases to save you time, money, and stress as well.

At that time, modern amenities were also roughed-in: all new plumbing, electrical wiring (naturally a first!) to replace the old, dodgy gas lights in the cabin with safer electric lights, and even a TV and satellite to connect us to the outside world when we wanted to be. The wiring carried to a new power box situated literally below-deck in the cellar, where a direct-wired gas generator (located in the Pelton wheel cabin eighty feet distant) would bring us power—using a remote on/off fob if we wished. Gary also set up, in case of an emergency or a breakdown, a manual plug-in override for a secondary generator backup to supply a bypass to the hard-wired one.

Phase IV. COMPLETION PHASE: INTERIOR WORK, LOWER CABINS REPAIRED

Though renovations took longer (always do) than forecast, we were blessed with an extremely mild winter—and light snowfall (six inches or less at a time) only several times that season, which melted so quickly it was of small consequence to our timetable.

Steve made use of snow days to fashion the loft stair components in his workshop, which he brought up pre-assembled. He also diligently continued making the time-consuming trek, often bringing Kirk, his lighthearted painter, to help finalize the job and seal frazzled nerves with his good-natured presence—*and* culinary skills. And as the existing partial-cupboards didn't make the cut, our cabinetmaker, Steve Wood, who'd made our home's cabinets, made the few hickory wood cabinets our tiny kitchen would hold.

Even then, he planned out the project around our old Servel fridge and O'Keefe and Merritt stove as though retrofitting a castle! Then our friend, tile mason Randy English, who laid the tile in our home, came up as well, driving the mountain road to tile our small kitchen counter and the newly carved out corner spot (tiled for safety under and around up to ceiling) for the new/used Lopi Endeavor woodstove (donated by dear friends who'd stored it as an unused "spare" in the cabin's garage), our only heat source that we can also cook on if need be. In a pinch we can also cook on our outdoor, wood-fueled fire pit (we have an unlimited wood supply on our property). This is what having friends, and a sense of cabin community, is all about. Items need not be new to be perfect. In fact, many things in our cabin were lovingly bestowed, or bought second-hand, lending (we feel) just the right ambiance to make it a real cabin. Beyond that, the bottom line on our bequeathed woodstove was that it was bulletproof and safe, unlike its burnt-out predecessor with its thumbtacked aluminum foil backing. And Randy wrapped up all his work in one day! But what a difference a day makes. It pays to have skilled

▶ A corner of the bedroom, after the remodel. The window at left opens to the deck, as do the two new windows at right.

▶ The kitchen view of our new hickory cabinets made by Steve Wood. The stove is a 1950 O'Keefe and Merritt.

◀ Randy English lays the tile for the spot where the woodstove will go. The second photo shows him laying tile for the kitchen sink area.

▶ We kept the original bathroom sink and cabinet.

craftsmen like Steve Wood and Randy, faithful friends who understand our needs.

Then as icing on the cake, I unearthed a heavy, old (1930s) cast-iron porcelain sink at an antique store for $35. At first glance, Gary was dubious, but he dove in, removing the old faucet that had literally frozen on after much muscle effort and two huge juxtaposed plumbing wrenches. After using a product called Amaz, I scrubbed and polished it to a gleam, revealing nary a scratch. But more hurdles needed jumping. It wasn't enough that I (with help) had to get that one-hundred-pound piece of iron into my vehicle on a rainy, muddy day, or that Gary had to strong arm the frozen faucet off, or that I rubbed it mar-less with the Amaz Creme face-lift. Next we had to heft it cabinward, present it to Steve, and cajole him into installing the thing. Nope. They sure don't make 'em like they used to—not only to last a lifetime, but to weigh like an anchor too. But change it? Never. It's gorgeous, and I'm proud of its origin, the result, and mostly the memories.

But talk about heavy—next, Steve hauled up the un-glam but oh-so-necessary new toilet and finally—*Ta-da!*—the new shower stall, with a repositioned shower entrance so one does not step into the toilet (as before) upon exiting. Now the left side of the stall formed a wall to the toilet and one could enter it straight on if desired by way of a newly cut in door, directly from our bedroom. We also had a secondary pocket door installed from our back porch hallway entry, so guests could also easily access the bathroom. It was also in this tiny bathroom that we successfully fought with the thin wall structuring limitations of the oldest portion of the original cabin to preserve the only existing original window mentioned earlier. Through its vintage top hinging, we can prop or hook it open for air and steam ventilation. Here also, we kept the forties vintage sink and cabinet, though the old faucet, puttied in place, needed removal, which Gary did. Here again, I spent several hours using more Amaz on the sink and the light-green Formica countertop, deemed a worthy effort as

◄ Original bathroom. The rusted metal shower was just removed.

◄ The new shower and toilet. The shower now faces out rather than toward the toilet.

▶ Ron Humphre, who did a tremendous amount of work for us when we were building our off-grid ranch, came up to the cabin and helped with stump removal and cleanup. He also helped dig out the soon-to-be-spring-fed pond below the cabin and lower orchard. Here he is operating his high-track D5, which is great for maneuevering in tight spots.

▶ Randy English cuts tile.

◄ My 1930s cast-iron sink. We installed new faucets and drain.

◄ The living room before the remodel. Note the gaslight hanging in the center.

▶ The remodeled living room, with the sliding door on the left, allowing direct access to the desk.

Gary said it shone like a new dime when finished. Still, his judgment was tested later when the light switch was flipped on and merciless brilliance from new light fixtures shone down on the glowing bathroom porcelain sink and on my kitchen sink. In fact, as our generator purred outside, we gave the entire inner sanctum a "pass!" Its unbiased grade: A+.

But I'm a bit ahead of myself. Before our final aced exam, the walls and ceilings needed repairs; and, when essential, replaced with new three-quarter-inch plywood, spaced so as to be finished at the seams, with two-inch slats that, once painted, emerged as though meant to be (not patched in) in what I, a novice, term very Adirondack-ish. And then, finally, Steve Downey got down on his hands and knees. Probably to thank God that he was almost done, but also to work on the flooring. To help him, he brought an expert in the art of hardwood laying to put down the thick (three-quarter-inch) hardwood flooring which we chose due to its strength and durability compared to a laminate or thinner board that might bow under the pressures of winter weather traffic. And, since we shopped about diligently, we procured (within our contract flooring budget) a durable-quality wood, marked way down because it was labeled a remnant.

These leftover crumbs are too small for most households—or rooms, especially with the waste factor. We bought every board, and bit our nails down to the last hammer blow. But as hoped, we were able to do the loft too, with wood to spare. That's where a skilled installer not only lays down floors that are lovely, and which are made to last a lifetime, but also saves cash, making it doubly lovely. The bottom line? No matter if you choose hardwood, tile, or even rough wood, as we considered, it pays to shop for quality and remnant prices. If need be, or if you have a larger area, consider other materials for each space. I know you're inventive. Put a custom brand on your retreat. And if your sense of flair raises eyebrows, just grin. Make it an original. Make it your own. But, make it secure too. Stock up on provisions just as in your prepped home so it's not only bodily, but mind and spirit comfortable too. The high R-F ratings you'll add (Relax Factors) will enhance your life and add years to it. Here's some R-F example ratings: There's a toasty fire, a fridge full of food, light fixtures to read by, and I just made comfort food: fudge anyone? But, feel free to factor in your own ways to *Relax*—to put your own personal R-F ratings right through the roof.

◀ Ron Humphrey roughing in the small reservoir below the cabin.

◀ The pond Gary built to capture water runoff from above. It filled in a day.

5. Water Renovations

Harnessing A Primary Survival Element
We'd had little time to put our feet up and relish a few of my walnut fudge chunks, as we had one more momentous project to see to: The cabin project was now done, but spring was waning to summer and it was a must for Gary to protect and purify our water system before our second winter set down around us. While he'd started planning this during breaks from the cabin redo, it was a huge project that needed undivided attention because of the critical need to build a good, constant water supply system that would require a low maintenance profile.

Earlier, he'd completed—with the help of friend and alternative power contractor, Bill Hasse (who'd implemented the off-grid power design Gary designed for our home)—the first and most critical phase of our water flow project. That would be the installation of a new 3000-gallon poly tank and water filtration system that allowed only filtered, purified water into the water-safe storage tank, through a stainless tank filtration system. So now it was time to bring these components to the spring area above the cabin. Gary pulled the huge, ungainly 3000-gallon tank up the mountain, secured by tie downs, in our only hauling trailer that, though small, performed glowingly due to its heavy-duty spring-loaded ramp. Upon arrival at the cabin, Gary unloaded the tank from the trailer, sliding it down the ramp and maneuvering it (with the help of his Honda ATV) up and around the steep logging road, into position on the tree-hidden plateau high above us. What a feat, especially as the tank tipped over and off the road at one time. Ultimately, this bought us precious time, as they had one day to temporarily join the new water and filtration tanks to the old existing line, then install an overflow line so when the tank filled, overflow went into an underground bypass line that Gary later dug down past and beyond the cabin, and would ultimately spill into the trout pond, irrigate a second orchard that we planted there (the deer and bears assume it's for them), and could supply running water to our timber claim cabin too.

▶ Gary enlisted his son, Andrew, along with Andrew's friend Ted Spencer and his son, Taryn, to help clean out the water tank storage area. The old galvanized tank is at left.

◄ Gary hired Rich Samson (who has a cabin in the area) to bring his Kubota L35 loader to clean off the staging area where the tank would go.

◄ Gary with the 3000-gallon tank after his escapade in getting up the steep hill, by himself. The filtration tank is next to it.

Prior to the install, during the cabin revamp, Gary had come up with his son Andrew and cleaned out the plateau area where the new tanks now rest. All the old tank timbers, originally built in the 1800s, had rotted partly into the ground, and more heavy timbers lay buried. The huge metal tank bands were there too (all metal was taken to the recycler), but the site was cleared and levelled by Gary's tractor float to prepare it for the tank's debut. If you need such work done and don't own a tractor, get access to this tool that does in minutes what would take days of work by two strong men.

From the tank site, the terrain slopes down steeply into another overgrown path we had to clear, where a galvanized line lay buried. The trail leads to an old orchard behind our cabin, then on down to the water mainline directly feeding into the earlier mentioned perpetual fountain in our yard. This line was to be tied into the new "Pex-lines" which Steve installed in the cabin basement. But, a brand-new water line stretching three hundred yards from the new tanks into the cabin Pex lines in the basement was needed and could not be put aside for the next season. First, it needed trenching, and only a hand trencher could get in to do the job on that steep slope. Renting one in town, Gary took friend Chip Gracey along for a day of trenching. Chip bought our walnut orchard and home five years earlier so he could move his family out of the city and revamp our hulling shop to a home office for his Rockland-based microchip corporation. That turn of events forced us into our first off-grid adventure twenty-five miles west, to our cattle ranch. But on this day, the plan was for Gary to trench while Chip held him from behind so he wouldn't career downhill as the heavy device dug, biting into the concrete earth all the while propelling him forward in one bone-jarring motion toward the cabin. After that, he trenched a line down to the pond. Chip was beside him all the way.

▶ Gary rented a trencher for the day, to trench from the 3000-gallon tank to the cabin. It's hard work, in steep terrain.

◄ Examples of the trenching distance and terrain. This path needed to be cleared before the trenching could begin. Distance: about 150 yards. Then Gary trenched about 150 yards from the cabin to the pond below the cabin, in order to lay in overflow line later.

◄ Gary also had to clear the pathway from the water tank that goes up to the spring head. The distance here was about 600 yards. A chainsaw, McLeod tool, lawn broom, and handwork were in order.

When Gary eventually laid in the new two-inch schedule 40 PVC line from the tank to the cabin, and made the connections so tank overflow poured directly into the pond, it created a split-off line just above the lower cabin. He capped it in case we wanted to plumb it; it was adjacent to the old Pelton wheel cabin. He also devised and installed two fire protection hydrants, including drain valves and nine hundred feet of fire hose. We unrolled the hoses as a precautionary measure, so they would be ready when we lit our two huge debris piles that would no doubt create huge blazes. We picked a damp day for the burning, and as the piles finally burned down, rain fell. I caught a snapshot of Gary reading a newspaper by a tiny campfire he'd started to keep us warm. As he read, lost in an article, he and the paper got soaked.

But coming back to the water system, with that stretch done and buried, it was time to put the rest of the plans into full swing, including replacing the whole crumbling aluminum pipe system to the spring. More than a quarter mile from the spring source to the tanks, it was compromised by fallen limbs, rocks, and debris and had leaks all along its length, despite the many makeshift repairs. The pipe, which carried the spring water from the springhead to that newly installed 3000-gallon tank, was not only rusted but

▲ The PVC pipe that crossed the pathway to make the connection to the tanks was eventually covered, so we could drive our ATV on the trail.

partly buried, so we feared it would crumble if we even attempted repairs. Following Gary's plan, we replaced it in a three-phase process.

Phase I: This phase involved clearing the perilous, overgrown trail to the spring. It needed clearing, as one could barely walk along it without slipping off the edge, especially in the rain or snow, and into a steep ravine. Gary cut down many trees around and even in the aluminum pipe. Some had two-inch trunks; others were a foot thick. Huge trees, fallen across the trail in the past, were rotting and lying across the path. Removal was systematic and direct as we worked from the old water tank, up the trail. The goal was to clear a swath wide enough so that an ATV could negotiate it. As Gary cut using two chainsaws, one large and a smaller backup saw, I moved along behind with Greta, throwing the cut-up trees and debris off to the side, with much of it going down into the ravine. The task was difficult to begin with, but we also had to take care so as not to break or dislodge the old above-ground aluminum water line, some of which was placed directly at the trail's center.

Phase II: The second phase involved detaching the ancient aluminum pipe and replacing it with ten-foot sections of schedule 40 two-inch PVC line. To get the piping to the site, we used our pipe trailer, a relic from Gary's walnut farming days, used to move large twenty-foot aluminum irrigation pipes. It had worked super when we hauled twenty-foot PVC sections from town for our home-site's water system five years before, but for this forty-mile jarring ride on a fairly wash-boarded road, we got the twenty foot sections banded in bundles of five. Once loaded on the pipe trailer, Gary cinched the tie-downs around them, and we were off—with extra cans of "hot-blue glue" to bond sections together and a horde of connective parts for all sorts of "what-if" scenarios. Our goal: A one-day remove-and-replace project. Though stopping often to tighten the straps, we finally arrived and parked the load at the tanks. Gary loosened the cinches and we began hefting each bundle (at one hundred-foot intervals) along the trail, beginning at the 3000-gallon tank. Soon we were at the spring's secondary juncture, a two-inch hefty rubber hose, wherein Gary would fasten a clamp around after fitting the two-inch PVC inside. But first he had to disconnect this two-inch hose from its primary juncture, the spring itself, where water is initially diverted. Thankfully this large hose line, running one hundred yards along a one-foot-wide footpath which we had also cleared) that connected into the aluminum pipe, did have to be replaced, only reattached to the new PVC line. After disengaging it, we tipped the hose line up and waited a few minutes as water along the line began to drain. There was no going back now as we began to break down the old line. One by one, we separated each rusted-out pipe section, carrying it to an area we'd chosen below the tanks to stockpile for posterity. Many had roots grown through and, as we pulled them free, pipe after pipe disintegrated. At times change isn't only good, but long overdue. We felt vindicated to have reckoned rightly over this ticking time bomb. With the twenty-foot aluminum section increments, it took no time to cover one-quarter mile. We stacked each discarded section in the pile we'd made against two well-placed bracing trees.

We worked swiftly as a team, as the smell of rain was in the air. While Greta "helped" me loosen the bundles and I began to lay them along the ditch area I'd cleared of leaves and duff on the path's inner edge, Gary used Christy's Red Hot Blue Glue to attach each PVC section to the next, gently laying them into that trailside makeshift gutter. Now there'd be no more pipeline at trail center, enabling the ATV to proceed unhindered from end to end. As we worked, it'd started to rain softly, and the freezing air caused frozen sleet to cover Greta's dense coat. She shook it off, and I put her in the pickup just as Gary finished the connections at both junctures: the two-inch hose at the far end and the one to the tanks. He then reconnected our water system at the spring to our new PCV line. It was finally done! Now all that remained was to test it out, which I did posthaste: I was chilled to the rafters in the sleety cold. Wet but elated, the three of us headed back to our comfy retreat warmed by our woodstove. I immediately hopped into the shower and it was gratifying when hot steamy water instantly gushed forth. I took a looong, hot, bone-thawing soak as my body had all but converted to an immovable iceberg.

Phase III: The final phase revamp did not happen until the following year, in the spring. It involved devising a protective cover to be fabricated and placed over the dammed-up spring. The existing "cover" consisted of an old eight-foot-long section of bent and rusty tin underlain with a screen mesh that together somewhat protected the channeled water from being clogged with leaves and debris as it entered into the two-inch hose through a two-foot cone-like filter attachment housed inside the dam area. The entire system was held down by a collection of boulders roughly the size of bowling balls. This meant that each time Gary went to check the spring or clean out the conical filter, he had to first remove all the debris on top and nearby, then the rocks, tin sheet, and finally the screening. To top it off, the entire system was set on a slope, making it hard to work around. Now, the new set-up was made up of a heavy metal fabricated top-plate, four feet wide by six feet long, that incorporated a three-by-three-foot door, which hinged backward. The front of the plate fit on top of the existing two-inch top lip of the front-facing three- by two-foot metal dam. Gary first had to dig out, widen, and level off the spring area to accommodate the new cover which he concreted in, then reinforced from both front and behind with rock and additional concrete. This eliminated the prior need to leak-proof the dam base with rags! Best of all, the old tin and rock weights are now gone. Gary designed the cover to be tamper-proof with a padlock, to prevent any two-footed predators from vandalizing anything. We had only one problem: The weight of the new metal cover was close to two hundred pounds. Though Gary devised a wooden travois fitted with two lawnmower wheels that we used once we slid the cover off our trailer, it was tough getting the cover onto the travois and chained to the Honda. Gary then cautiously negotiated up the back road, with me behind to adjust the load, and stop the binding from slipping and the load from listing. I held my breath as we passed the tanks and climbed the steep hill to our newly carved ATV path and the final one-quarter mile to the two-inch hose juncture. There we slid it off and laid it on the bank to await further manpower: It would take two to three men to sidestep not only the awkward, lidded metal cover along the one-hundred-yard-long, one-foot-wide shale-banked path I'd widened a bit, but also to heft thirty sixty-pound sacks of concrete across it. Gary enlisted son Andrew and his friend Ted to this end, and they both also helped in mixing the concrete in a wheelbarrow. Then, together, they all set the new cover in place atop the covered dirt ledges Gary had chiseled out earlier. The predator-proof metal guard fit perfectly. Better yet, it took just a lid-lift for year-round "spring cleaning." And this is the name of the game for us: High maintenance turned to low maintenance. That, coupled with increased fortification of the water system against the weather and predators such as bears and wild hogs, led to an overall long-term bulletproof water flow guarantee. (Translation: When the snow and ice line the trail to the spring, we don't have to check it for problems unless we want to. Even in winter, the dangerous challenge the pathway presented is gone and it is now a pleasure to traverse. Plus we get unlimited cold spring water or a hot shower with the turn of the faucet.)

6. Electricity

In today's technology-driven world, power is an all but survivalist essential, even if one can live without it. That said, we wanted power in some form at our retreat. Thankfully, we didn't have to worry about needing electricity to run a pump for running water, as we now had a refurbished gravity-flow water system. We did, however, ponder using the running water to power some form of electricity. It was quite doable, as the vertical drop-off needs tested positive through a method that Gary had used years earlier, when building reservoirs on our ranch with his D-7 Caterpillar. Though there is a hose-tube and funnel method—described in detail on the site below—I feel the following is easier and more feasible—at least in our case. What Gary did was incrementally measure the watercourse route with a hand-held level as I stepped it off, marking each ten-foot increase for him to move to (he jotted down each one and later multiplied that total by ten to decide total feet of drop incline) before I walked ahead and upward. Below are examples from energy.gov of what such a system could look like. At right is a brushless Micro Hydro Unit From Hydro Induction Power at www.homehdro.com that offers many system setup examples:

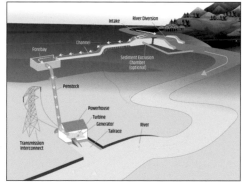

Courtesy of U.S. Department of Energy

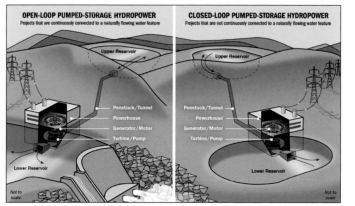

Courtesy of U.S. Department of Energy

In our case, as the Forebay shown in the diagram, our property's creek headwater and the 'powerhouse' is the actual original tiny powerhouse or Pelton wheel or overshot water wheel cabin I explained was built for this purpose a century earlier by a logging firm. To recreate this historical system was appealing to us, with a brand-new wheel motor, not unlike the original late 1800s motor that Gary and Andrew unearthed. However, the new one would be smaller, more fitted to our needs, and highly effective. The thought was so cool we could taste it.

However, things don't always go as planned. After serious debate, and weighing factors such as water rights permitting (though we have first water rights), and despite the fact that the plan called for recycling water flow directly back to the creek, we realized we may not be there often enough to maintain it properly. We consequently shelved the idea on this remarkable alternative, at least for a while.

We eventually decided to rebuild the Pelton wheel using one of the few boards left from the original wheel as a template, and installed the 350-pound eight-foot wheel on the existing shaft exactly where it had been originally attached to the Pelton wheel cabin. Gary had a friend and the wheel's reconstructer first help install it on new framework built onsite and attached alongside the small cabin. However, just getting the wheel there without shaking apart took forethought: Gary used a flatbed trailer lined with hay bales to create a flat padded surface to lay the wheel on and cushion its bumpy ride.

So now the wheel was installed, but it remained stationary. We wanted to see that wheel turn again. So what did we do? In October, Gary had transported his bulldozer up to clean the roads within our property, as well as the one coming into it. After a close call with a huge lightning strike forest fire coming within a quarter mile of our cabin, he also did some other work around

◀ The original Pelton wheel cabin.

▶ Refurbishing the Pelton wheel cabin, underway. Note the state of the original Pelton wheel. The window at front is one of the original cabin windows.

▶ Jim Maki made the trip up to help Gary with the wheel install. He is an engineer who also designed the model and template for the rebuilding of the wheel that is on the original shaft. All of the hardware—including the shaft, plating, bearings, square-headed nuts, and bolts—is original.

◀ Closeup of the Pelton wheel cabin.

◀ This is the large ring gear attached to the Pelton wheel. There is also a small pinion gear that was originally attached to the shaft that ran the original model (patented August 2, 1881) seen in front.

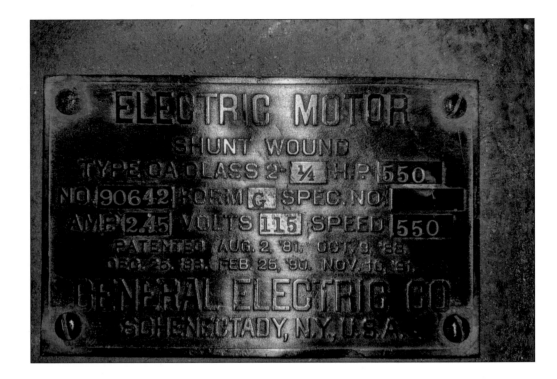

▶ Closeup of plate attached to motor.

the cabin, including digging out a little pond directly below our rebuilt Pelton wheel. Why do that when we had already decided not to trench a water pipeline from Maple Creek, which ran above and through our property? Where would the water source come from? We did have that steep pipeline adjacent to the Pelton wheel cabin, which Gary had also trenched when doing a line to our cabin. This was intended to handle overflow directly from the 3000-gallon water tank holding our spring water. This secondary line was just *sitting* there, held under extreme pressure with a shut off valve. It was crying out, "Use me you fools!" All we needed to do was create a "Y" hose bib (so we could still multipurpose that water source) and thread a twenty-five-foot hose line directly through the Pelton wheel cabin itself, then elbow it down through the wall and let the water cascade over the wheel. We hooked it up on October 28, 2019. And how did it work? With very little water flow, we had the wheel turning, channeling water below the wheel and into

the pond, with overflow going back into Maple Creek through twenty-foot PVC sections. Later we hope to install a motor to the Pelton wheel shaft if it will in fact generate enough power. So without extra trenching, water diversion, and worries tied to that hurdle, our water wheel is spinning smoothly and true after more than one hundred years of non-use.

We wanted a hydro plant, we planned for one, and now it may (or may not) happen. We'll see. I explain it here, as you too will have such trials and setbacks in your quest for preparedness if you pursue the dream of a getaway cabin. Use them, as we did, to your advantage and go on. Let it rest a while and take it on from another angle (as we did) if you can. A hydro plant can work for you, but weigh all the options and know that nothing worth having is easy. You must first determine its feasibility: Is the vertical distance (head) available and is there enough flow of the water? Enough falling water must be available, which usually, but not always, means hilly or mountainous sites are best.

◀ The new Pelton wheel in place, with water running to it. Note the water spilling from the pipe, above left.

◀ Backside of the Pelton wheel cabin. We placed the railroad tie steps and brought the cedar posts (circa 1880) from our ranch that Gary used to tie off the rope railing. The small, elbowed white PVC pipe that is just visible from the ground in center right is the water line we tied into, to bring water to the wheel.

▶ Another view of the inside of the Pelton wheel cabin. Note our Champion generator with remote start—all we had to do was press a fob to get the cabin up and running. The old generator at left has been refurbished, and is now used as a backup.

▶ Gary brought his D5 Caterpillar to the cabin to work on roads around the property as well as to make firebreaks and clean up where needed. Here, he takes the time out to dig a pond for the water wheel watershed.

▲ Here is the small reservoir I refined and cleaned up after Gary dug out the basic area. Above it is the water pathway I dug out by hand that went under the Pelton wheel down into it.

◄ Here, I line the spillway with rock that we gathered from down the road. Much of it has chrome in it. Chrome was mined in this geologically rich area more than ninety years ago.

▲ Water spilling into the pond holding area. The PVC pipe, elbowed down into the water at right, drains the pond before it overflows. The overflow line runs downhill 100 yards and the water drains back into Maple Creek which flows through our property.

▶ This is where we tied into the water line and buried the hose under the pathway before bringing it up into the Pelton cabin and feeding it out the other side.

Other factors for a micro-hydro site include its power output, economics, permits, and water rights. Next you need find out if the power you can get from flowing water on your site is enough. Here's how:

1) Calculate Head—the vertical distance the water falls (described above).
2) Calculate Flow—the quantity of water falling (bucket method below).

Once you've calculated head and flow, apply a simple equation to estimate power output for 53 percent efficiency, which is typical of most hydro systems. Multiply net head (vertical distance available after subtracting losses from pipe friction) by flow (gallons per minute) divided by 10. That'll give you system output in watts (W). It's simpler than it seems. The equation looks this: net head (feet) × flow (gpm)] ÷ 10 = W (watts).

▲ Above left is the installation diagram; at right is the 50gpm intake system with two-inch pipe.

Determining the "Head" Part of That EQ at Your Potential Site: Low or High

Most hydro sites are classified as low or high head. The higher the head, the better it is. Why? You need less water to produce a given amount of power and you can use smaller, less expensive equipment. Low head refers to a change in elevation of less than ten feet. A vertical drop of less than two feet will probably make a small-scale hydroelectric system unfeasible. Still, for very small power generation amounts, a flowing stream with as little as thirteen inches of water can support a submersible turbine. Also, when determining head, remember that you need to consider both *gross and net* head. While from above, you now know gross head is the vertical distance between the top of the penstock that conveys water under pressure and the point where the water discharges from the turbine, while net head equals gross head minus losses due to friction and turbulence in the piping. An alternative power expert or surveyor can help you here.

Determining "Flow" Part of Above EQ at a Potential Microhydropower Site

The quantity of water falling from a potential hydropower site is called flow. It's measured in gallons per minute, cubic feet per second, or liters per second. One easy way to resolve your stream's flow is to obtain data from these local offices:

1. US Geological Survey
2. US Army Corps of Engineer
3. US Dept. of Agriculture
4. Your county engineer
5. Local water supply/flood control officials.

Bucket Method To Measure Water Flow

If you can't get existing data, you'll need to conduct your own flow measurements, which we did using the easy bucket method, which involves damming your stream with rocks, logs, or boards to divert flow into a bucket. The rate it fills is the flow rate: A five-gallon bucket that fills in one minute = your stream's flow to be five *gallons* per minute.

Economics, Permits, Water Rights, and Government Control

If you determine from your estimated power output that a microhydropower system is feasible, then you can determine whether it makes sense economically. Add up all the estimated costs of developing and maintaining the site over the expected life of your equipment, then divide the amount by the system's capacity in watts. This will tell you how much the system will cost in dollars per watt. Then compare that to the cost of other alternative power sources. Whatever the upfront costs, a hydroelectric system will typically last a long time and, in many cases, maintenance is not expensive. In addition, sometimes there are a variety of financial incentives available on the state, utility, and federal level for renewable energy system investments. They include income tax credits, property tax exemptions, state sales tax exemption, loan programs, and special grant programs.

Then, you need to learn local permit requirements and water rights. If your system will have minimal environmental impact, and you're not planning to sell power to a utility (our idea was to be remote and off-grid), the permitting process will likely involve minimal effort. But, if exposed to permitting (assess its locale and size), your first contact should be the county engineer and the state energy office, who can provide you with advice and assistance. From these agencies, you'll find the divertible water amount. And

as each state controls water rights; you may need a separate water right to produce power, even if you now have other water rights.

What Are We Doing for Power?

Though solar and battery power may be a cost effective option in years to come, we wanted to go into relax mode now but still have electricity. The solution was to use two generators for power, with the second being a backup. Why? Relative to solar and hydro power, generator power is an inexpensive, direct, portable, and fool-proof option, especially when you have a backup gen. Plus, it's low maintenance. As the primary power source, we chose a remote-start Champion 3500-4000-watt model that we could easily move around or transport. We placed it inside the Pelton wheel cabin and can still start and stop it with the paired fob from our cabin at over eighty feet (eighty being the given top operating distance) away. Lightweight (one hundred pounds) and portable, it comes with a handle and wheel kit and performs quietly, even at close range. It's also fuel efficient, running twelve hours on a tank (3.8 gallon) of gas. We bought ours through Home Depot for less than $500.

A couple of tips. Tip 1: Gary often buys airplane fuel in five-gallon jugs at our local airport, as this gas runs clean and will not clog the carburetor if left undrained for a length of time—saving on costly or time-consuming repairs and cleaning out of fuel plug-ups. However, if you're planning not to use your generator for a period of time (say over the winter) and if you drain the system completely, normal fuel is fine to use. To lengthen fuel life from its normal six-month span to possibly two years, use a fuel additive called *STA-BIL*. Tip 2: Have a backup generator on hand. It doesn't have to be a powerhouse, but one that will allow you to function normally or close to it, while the other is down. We have a real little workhorse to do this job, a Honda 2000 gas-powered inverter generator. Completely portable, one can pick up this fifty-pounder by its handle and tote it anywhere. We simply plug it into the secondary outlet we had wired to the fuse box and can use it in lieu of the Champion. It is super economical and quiet and can run for eight hours on a gallon of fuel. We used it for a year while living in our trailer when our house was being built, and it was 100 percent dependable. Drawbacks include the fact that there is no remote stop/start on this model and, due to inverter sine-wave technology, it costs double the Champion. I saw one online recently on sale for $899. Following are the nitty-gritty statistics for both.

The Champion Generator Statistics:

- RV ready—equipped with std. 30-amp RV outlet, enough power to run a 15,000-BTU RV a/c.
- 4000 starting watts, 3500 running watts with up to twelve hours run time on a full tank of gas.
- Powered by a reliable 196cc Champion engine with wireless remote start, up to eighty feet away.

- Outlets—120-volt 30-amp locking, 120-volt 30-amp RV, 120-volt 20-amp household outlets all secured by volt guard, protects your appliances from power surges.
- Champion support—three-year limited warranty with free lifetime technical support.
- 68 dBA at twenty-three feet, auto-choke for one-touch starts, low-oil shut-off sensor.
- USDA-approved spark arrestor, one-inch-durable tubular steel frame, EPA approved; forty-nine states.
- Includes remote, wheel kit, oil funnel, (SAE 10-30W is recommended) spark plug socket/battery.

Honda 2000 Generator Statistics

- Clean, consistent power for microwaves, refrigerators, hair dryers, small air-conditioning units, C-Pap machines, and much more: this popular model can operate a wide variety of appliances as well, making it super useful, lightweight (under forty-six pounds), compact, and portable.

- Runs up to eight hours on under a gallon of fuel, making it great for overnight power.
- Advanced inverter technology—reliable power for computers and other sensitive equipment. Honda's inverter technology means stable, clean power in a smaller, lighter package. The precision of Honda's inverter technology ensures our inverter generators produce power that is as reliable as the power you get from your outlets at home.
- Double power with parallel capability: Get an optional cable/cord for 4,000-watt power.
- 12-volt, 8.0-amp unregulated DC output: use when charging 12-volt automotive-type batteries (requires an optional charging cord).
- Oil alert: Engine shuts off when a low oil level is detected.
- Three-year residential and commercial warranty.

Honda 3000iS (pull start, around $2000; electric start, $2300)

Statistics: In addition to all the above, the Honda 3000iS is equipped with Honda's exclusive Eco-Throttle System, runs from 7.2 to twenty hours on a single tank (3.4 gallons) of fuel depending on load, and the Eco-Throttle™ allows the generator's engine to automatically adjust the engine speed to produce only the power needed. It can also be paralleled to 6000W power. A wireless remote control kit is sold separately (Pinellas Power Products is a top example) at www.pinellaspowerproducts.com for about $350.

But now you can see how easy it is to bring power to your getaway spot with only a generator. I bet you didn't think it could be so easy. You can always add solar power and build your own water wheel for water retrieval—if you choose—on one of those long summer days when you grow "tired" of just relaxing on your own retreat's porch.

▲ Our new Honda EU2200 generator, pictured at our home.

7. Building a Basic Off-Grid System

hile living off-grid may change your lifestyle, the transition can be seamless if you do some upfront planning, such as being aware of the power you and your family are currently consuming. That is as easy as checking your monthly utility bills. Also, be aware that some appliances, such as an air-conditioning unit (which needs a generator to handle the start load), require more power to run. Other than that, a generator should really only be necessary to boost your battery bank in the short days of winter and also under extended cloud cover conditions. A good-sized system of solar panels will mitigate the need to burn fuel in your generator as the more energy brought in through the system each day, the merrier it will be, showing "Full" on your monitoring device for a longer period of time—in particular, in winter and spring. This also extends battery life, as when the batteries hold a charge longer (above 80 percent), they retain a cycle. See a detailed explanation of cycles and battery life in my *HOW TO BUILD THE PERFECT OFF-GRID HOME, Let the Sun Rain Down on Your Solar* (Second Edition).

How a Solar System Works Off-Grid

A photo-voltaic (PV) system consists of panels that convert sunlight into electricity, a charge controller to prevent the batteries from overcharging, a set of batteries to store the electricity for when the sun is not shining, and an inverter to flip the low-voltage DC (battery voltage) into 120 volts AC house current.

Solar Panels (PV)

There are many ways to mount solar panels. Some of these methods may include fixed on your roof, fixed on the ground, fixed on pole mounts, or pole-mounted tracking arrays. Mounting your panels on the roof makes sense from a security, stealth, and convenience standpoint, and can lower roof temperatures in hot climates, but is inconvenient in snow country. Panel angle needs seasonal adjustment for best collection. According to AltEnergyMag.com, consider the size of a 200-watt panel when weighing the mounting location options: It is approximately 60 inches x 40 inches x 1.5 inches, and weighs about forty pounds.

Charge Controller

The solar panels can only do their duty after they're wired to a charge controller, which feeds batteries the proper electric dosage, at a rate they can handle. It also ensures a longer battery life. In the past, grouping of components revolved around a 12v solar panel, a 12v charge controller, and a 12v battery. Now it is common to see a more efficient series string of panels running at a higher voltage (at least 20v higher than battery voltage), a special MPPT controller, and the

▼ One of two ground-mounted solar panels found at our off-grid home.

12v battery pack. The MPPT controller can match optimal panels to batteries' performance, allowing up to a 30 percent power increase according to AltEnergyMag.com, *without needing more panels*.

Batteries

Many off-grid systems use a flooded lead acid (deep cycle) battery. We have four large HUP (High Utilization Positive) Solar-Ones at our off-grid home.

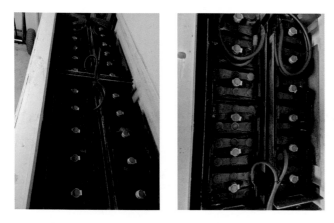

▲ Our HUP Solar One battery bank in our off-grid home.

The unit has vented caps, discharges hydrogen during charging, and needs to be vented, as well as have water added. Our HUP Solar-One battery bank requires a drink twice a month in summer and every other month in winter. You will also need to equalize the batteries every two to three months as part of battery health.

However, AGM battery types do not need venting, and are sealed, eliminating the need to add water. They also won't leak acid when damaged, although they are pricier than the HUP varieties. Battery sizes are 6v and 12v. One needs: two 6v in series to be a 12v, four in series for a 24v system, or eight in series for a 48v system. Paralleling multiple 12v batteries (or 6v pairs) ups amp hour storage (i.e., two 100ah batteries in parallel=200ah). Batteries in series add voltage; in parallel, amp hours.

Inverter

An inverter changes low voltage DC (direct current) into 120v AC (alternating current) and since all our household appliances need ac to operate, an inverter comes in handy. Inverters can, according to AltEnergyMag.com, range from a $60 Wal-Mart 750-watt Black and Decker, to a $2500 Xantrex or Outback with integrated battery charger and transfer switch for connecting to a generator—or tying it into the grid. Note: An inexpensive inverter definitely has its application, as it can be wired directly to an appliance. Larger units like the Outback variety, which we purchased, connect directly to the whole enchilada—your breaker panel.

Fuses, Breakers, and Disconnects

Another important additive for safety and expediency: Install fused disconnects between the solar panels and the charge controller, between the charge controller and batteries, and between the batteries and the inverter. Why? One can zero in on components in need of maintenance (or panel placement), or automatically disconnect in case of a short or equipment malfunction.

Battery Monitor

After investing all that time and money into your setup, you want to know how much energy you have in reserve, or if you need to boost the power by flipping on the generator. The best method is an amp hour meter wired to your battery pack to indicate amp hours stored and used. These units commonly also include an amp and voltmeter function. There are standalone units like the Bogart Trimetric and integrated units like the Outback Flexnet DC.

Wire Size

Wire size is a function of amps being carried (in other words, it gets your power from point A to B) and the distance they need to move. Again, per AltEnergyMag.com, if you have 40 amps (480 watts) of PV on your roof, and it's eight feet to the charge controller and batteries, then you should use 8 AWG

(American wire gauge/brown & sharpe) wire between the PV panels and the charge controller (and from charge controller to batteries). The wires between your battery and inverter should be short and large: a 2000-watt inverter, six feet from the battery bank, needs one AWG battery cable—and the smaller the AWG, the larger the cable. If your cables are too small, they will generate heat, possibly start a fire, and drop the voltage into the dirt. Altenergymag suggests using the calculator at the bottom of www.powerstream.com/Wire_Size.htm and use 3 percent voltage drop (or less) as target.

More On Generators

Many northern climates have a large number of sunless days. As said, we like the Honda EU series generators. They are small, quiet, and scalable (can run one for small loads, and save a second for heavy loads). Yamaha makes a similar series. Both can be modified to run on gasoline and/or propane. This is where you'll want the better inverter/charger/transfer units as mentioned in the inverter section, as there is just one cable to connect to the generator, and switching/charging is automatic. A wired or wireless remote is available for remote start and shutdown, and pricier inverters handle this procedure automatically based on battery needs.

Sizing the system

I'll try keeping this simple. A 200-watt panel in New York, optimally aligned (solar south, at an angle similar to latitude with seasonal adjustments), might gather 600 watt hours daily (three full sun hours—200w); in California it may get 1200 watt hours (six full sun hours—200w). By the way, 1200-watt hours is enough energy to run a 100-watt light bulb for twelve hours. See the pattern? Fortunately, we have better options than a 100-watt light bulb. In our home, we initially installed 14-watt CFL's (compact fluorescent lights). They supply similar light to an old 80-watt incandescent light bulb and use way less energy. In fact, one has to look very hard to even find an incandescent light bulb anymore.

Some basic formulas

Volts x Amps = Watts
Watts x Hours = Watt Hours
Watt Hours / Volts = Amp Hours
Amp x Hours = Amp Hours

For detailed information on how to convert (it will do it for you automatically) electric current in amps to electric current in watts, go to RapidTables at www.rapidtables.com. (There are many online options.)

A battery rated at 100ah has about 50ah usable (50 percent discharge); otherwise, if more are used, its life could be severely degraded. Typically, batteries are rated at the C/20 rate, where a 100ah battery might deliver five amps for twenty hours. Taking into account the 50 percent discharge, you are looking at 5 amps for ten hours. If you pull the amp hours out faster, you have fewer usable ah; conversely, at a slower rate, you have more usable ah. More sizing info and a chart showing sun hours for various areas is found at www.green-trust.org/2003/pvsizing/default.htm; while a calculator for battery and solar sizing can be found at http://www.green-trust.org/peukert/.

More on Loads and Run Times

A 700-watt (cooking watts) microwave may pull down 1000 watts. If used for fifteen minutes, it consumes 250-watt hours. A 30-watt laptop computer used for four hours consumes 120-watt hours. A kilowatt meter is for monitoring the amps, watts, and watt-hour consumption of 120vac devices, and can be found for around $20 at Radio Shack, Amazon.com, and other places. There are similar devices for measuring 12vdc loads. I outline an extensive appliance watt-hours usage chart in my previous book, *HOW TO BUILD THE PERFECT OFF-GRID HOME, Let The Sun Rain Down On Your Solar (Second Edition)* (along with power calculation methods) under the chapter about appliances and lighting.

Putting It All Together: Here Is How You Do It

Now that you have mounted the panels on the roof or on a yard mount, you'll want to connect them in parallel (unless using the MPPT controller, as its panel and controller specific; check the data sheets for both). Keep array voltage below 100v. Connect positive to positive (red) and negative to negative (black), and then bring the wires inside to the charge controller (remember, series adds voltage, parallel adds amps). Don't forget your fused disconnect between the panels and charge controller.

Next connect the charge controller to the batteries. Again, it›s positive-to-positive (red) and negative-to-negative (black), with a fused disconnect in between.

Next connect the batteries to the inverter. Again, it's positive-to-positive, negative-to-negative, with a fused disconnect in between. If you are using a 24v or 48v battery pack, wire four or eight 6v batteries in series, respectively. You will need special controllers and inverters for the higher voltages, but your battery cables will be much smaller in large systems. This is the type of installation where a MPPT controller like the Outback FM 60/80 really shines.

What's It Going to Cost?

A basic low-end system might consist of a 200-watt panel ($550), a 20-amp charge controller ($100), two Wal-Mart-type 27 marine deep-cycle 12v batteries ($160), and a Wal-Mart 750-watt inverter ($60). With miscellaneous wires, fuses, and connectors, you are looking at just under $1000 for an autonomous, gridless (no power bill) power system. You would, as an example, be able to power a couple of lights, a radio, and a small RV water pump, ideal for a rainwater collection system.

A slightly larger setup might consist of 400 watts of PV ($1100), a 40-amp charge controller ($150), 200ah of Deep Cycle (two Trojan T-105 6v's) battery storage ($300), and a 2000-watt inverter/charger ($1700). With various wires, fuses, and connectors, costs are about $3000. This allows some use of a TV or laptop, and a microwave, which needs a lot of power. If you are looking at a total whole house off-grid system (i.e. 4500w), the costs go up exponentially depending on your components and personal power needs.

Appropriate Energy Use To Conserve Electricity

To reduce power consumption, propane appliances like the kitchen stove and refrigerator, water heater, clothes dryer, and furnace are common. However, this is just shifting you to the propane grid, although propane can be stored indefinitely. Another alt-energy solution is wood-fired, for heat and cooking (see description starting on page 79 on how Jill in Australia has done this for thirty years); wood- or solar-heated hot water; use of indoor/outdoor clothes lines instead of a mechanical dryer; rainwater harvesting; a cistern instead of a deep well; and composting toilets instead of flush toilets. Jill uses her "Dunny," the old-fashioned outhouse method. It's plain and simple.

A DIY Nine-Step Off-Grid Solar Setup

Below I have included a basic Nine-Step DIY solar setup as some may find it helpful as a guideline to follow.

According to engineer Debasish Dutta from Walden Labs, if you've decided to install a small solar panel system for home power needs, this "tutorial" is helpful. Walden Labs is a sharing place for building self-reliance and resilience, and learning about the survival skills of our ancestors, homesteading, preparedness, and decentralization. They strive to help people of all experience levels take steps towards happier, healthier, and more self-reliant lives.

In this basic prototype. Dutta provides a step-by-step guide to buying different components and wiring everything by yourself, though he says, "You must know some basic electrical and math for designing the entire system." (I agree. If not, get some help.) For an off-grid solar system, you need four basic components:

1. Solar Panel (PV Panel)
2. Charge Controller
3. Inverter
4. Battery

Besides the above components, you need a few more things such copper wire, MC4 connector, breaker, meter and fuses, and so on.

Note about parts: The picture below shows a big solar panel of 255W @ 24V, two batteries of 12V @ 100Ah each, 30A @ 12/24V PWM solar charge controller, and a 1600 VA pure sine wave inverter. During the calculation, he took a smaller solar system example for better understanding.

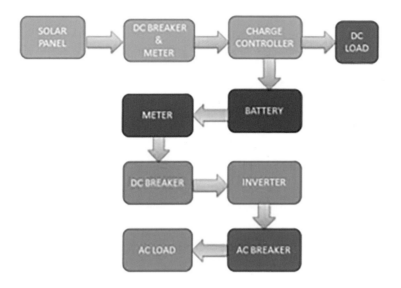

▲ Diagram above shows how the charge controller should be wired.

Step 1: Load Calculation

Before choosing the components, you have to calculate your power load, how much time it will run, etc. It is simple to calculate if you know basic math.

1. Decide appliances (light, fan, TV) you want to run and for how many hours.
2. See the specification chart in your appliances for power rating.
3. Calculate the Watt Hour, which is equal to the product of the power rating of your appliances and run time (hours). Load Calculation Example: Let's say you want to run a 11W compact fluorescent lamp (CFL) for five hours from a solar panel, then the watt hour is equal to:

Watt Hour: 11W x 5 hr = 55

4. Calculate the total watt hour: Just as with the CFL we'll now calculate the watt hour for all the appliances and add them together. Example:

CFL = 11W x 5 hr = 55

Fan = 50 W x 3hr = 150

TV = 80W x 2hr = 160

Total Watt Hours = 55+150+160 = 365

Now that the load calculation is over, the next thing is to choose the right components to match your load requirement. If you are not interested in doing the above math, then use a load calculator for this calculation. There are many such load calculators available on the internet, such as the "Off-Grid Load Calculator."

Step 2: Battery Selection

The output from the solar panel is DC power. This power is generated during daytime only. So if you want to run a DC load during daytime, then it seems to be very easy. But doing this is not a good decision for two reasons:

1. Most of the appliances need a constant rated voltage to run efficiently. Solar panel voltage is not constant; it varies according to the sunlight.
2. If you want to run the appliances during the night, then it is impossible.

Using a battery to store the solar power during the day solves the above problem. It will provide a constant source of stable, reliable power.

There are various kinds of batteries. Car and bike batteries are designed for supplying short bursts of high current and then need to be recharged and are not designed for a deep discharge. But the solar battery is a deep-cycle lead-acid battery that allows for partial discharge and for deep, slow discharge. Lead acid tubular batteries are perfect for a solar system. Ni-MH batteries and Li-Ion batteries are also used in many small power applications.

Note: Before going to choose the components, decide your system voltage; is it 12/24 V or 48 V? The higher the voltage, the lesser the current and the lesser the copper loss will be in the conductor. This will also reduce your conductor size. Most of the small home solar systems will have 12 V or 24 V. In the description of his project Debasiash says, "I've selected the 12 V system."

Rating of Battery

Battery capacity is rated in terms of Ampere hour:
Power = voltage x current
Watt Hour = voltage (volts) x current (amperes) x time (hours)
Battery Voltage = 12V (as in the 12V-system example)
Battery capacity = load/voltage = 365/12 = 30.42 Ah

But batteries are not 100 percent efficient, so assuming 80 percent efficiency:

Capacity = 30.42/0.8 = 38.02 Ah

Therefore, if one allows a *small* margin—voila! One can select a 40Ah deep-cycle lead-acid battery.

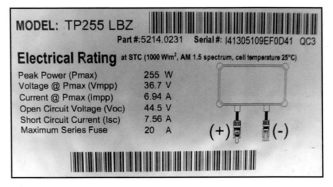

Step 3: Solar Panel Selection

The solar panel converts the sunlight into electricity as direct current (DC). These panels are typically categorized as monocrystalline or polycrystalline. Monocrystalline panels are costlier and more efficient than polycrystalline panels. Solar panels are generally rated under standard test conditions (STC): Irradiance of 1,000 W/m², solar spectrum of AM 1.5, and module temperature at 25°C. (That sure is handy to know isn't it? Or is it?)

Rating of Solar Panel

The solar panel size should be selected in such a way that it will charge the battery fully in one sunny day. During the twelve hours of daytime, the sunlight is not uniform, and it also differs according to your location on the globe. So we can assume four hours of effective sunlight that will generate the rated power.

So total power output of panels = 12V x 40Ah
= 480Wh

Power to be generated per hour = 480 / 4 = 120W

Again, by taking some margin one can choose a 125W, 12v solar panel.

Step 4: Charge Controller Selection

A solar charge controller is a device that is placed between a solar panel and a battery. It regulates the voltage and current coming from your solar panels. It is used to maintain the proper charging voltage on the batteries. As the input voltage from the solar panel rises, the charge controller regulates the charge to the batteries, preventing any overcharging.

Usually, the solar power system uses 12-volt batteries, although solar panels can deliver far more voltage than is required to charge the batteries. Thus, by converting the excess voltage into amps, the charge voltage can be kept at an optimal level while the time required to fully charge the batteries is reduced—allowing the solar power system to operate optimally at all times.

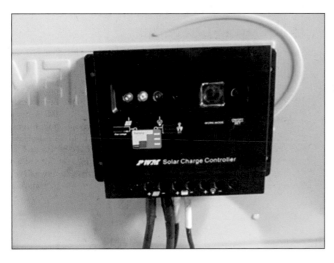 

▲ Two examples of charge controllers.

Types of Charge Controllers and Rating of Charge Controller

1. ON/OFF
2. PWM
3. MPPT

Try to avoid the ON/OFF charge controller, as it is the least efficient. Among the three, MPPT offers the highest efficiency but it's pricy. So you can use either PWM or MPPT.

Since our example system is rated at 12 volts, the charge controller is also 12 volts. The current rating = power output of panels /voltage which = 125 W / 12V = 10.4 A. So in this case, choose a charge controller of 12 volts and more than 10.4 amps.

Step 5: Inverter Selection

▲ Debasiash's 1600 VA pure sine wave inverter.

Solar panels (PV) receive the sun's rays and convert them into electricity called direct current (DC). DC is then converted into alternating current (AC) through a device called an inverter. AC electricity flows through every outlet of our homes.

Inverter Types

1. Square Wave
2. Modified Sine Wave
3. Pure Sine Wave

Square Wave inverters are cheapest but not suited for all appliances. Modified Sine Wave output is also unsuitable for certain appliances, chiefly those with capacitive and electromagnetic devices: a fridge, microwave, and most kinds of motors. Typically modified sine wave inverters work at lower efficiency than pure sine wave inverters. In Debasiash's opinion, a Pure Sine Wave inverter is the best choice, and I absolutely agree.

The inverter may be grid tied or standalone. In our case, our pure sine wave inverters are standalone as we are off the grid—and as far as I'm concerned are a necessity.

Rating of Inverter

The power rating should be equal or more than the total load in watt at any instant. In the example, the maximum load at any instant for the three items being powered: TV (50W) + Fan (80W) + CFL (11W) = 141W. With some margin we can choose a 200W inverter. For our 12V example, we have to select a 12V DC to 230V/50Hz or 110V/60Hz AC pure sine wave inverter.

Note: *Appliances such as refrigerators, hair driers, vacuum cleanesr, washing machines, and so on, are likely to have a starting power consumption several times greater than their normal working power (typically this is caused by electric motors or capacitors in such appliances). This should be taken into account when choosing the right size of inverter.*

Step 6: Mounting the Solar Panel and Preparing the Mounting Stand

After designing the solar system, buy all components with appropriate rating as per the previous five steps.

Now it is time to mount the solar panel. First choose a suitable location on the rooftop, or ground, with no obstruction of sunlight. You can make your own stand or buy one. In the example shown below, Debasiash had taken the drawing from the solar panel company and made it at a nearby welding shop. The tilt of his stand is near equal to the latitude angle of his location.

▲ The stand for his big solar panel.

He made a small wooden mounting stand for his 10-watt solar panel. (See photo below.)

▲ The small wooden mounting stand for the 10-watt panel.

Tilting

To get the most from solar panels, you need to point them in the direction that captures the maximum sunlight—for example, south if you're in the northern hemisphere, or north if you're in the southern hemisphere. With non-stationary, adjustable panel arrays you are able to follow the seasons and move your arrays. One must also optimize the horizontal angle relative to the ground. To do so, Debasiash says to use one of these formulas to find the best panel tilt angle from the horizontal:

• If your latitude is below 25 degrees, use the latitude times 0.87.
• If your latitude is between 25 and 50 degrees, use the latitude, times 0.76, plus 3.1 degrees.

First, place the stand in such a way that the face is directed toward the south (or north, if you're in the southern hemisphere). Mark the leg position over the roof.

To get the south/north direction, use the compass android app or a real compass. He decided to secure his 255W solar panel mount on his roof with concrete. He roughened up the surface at each leg of the stand and made a one-square-foot rough surface on the roof at each leg. This is helpful for perfecting the bonding between the roof and concrete.

Now one needs to mix the concrete and mount the panels to the stand: First, prepare the concrete by mixing the cement and stones.

Prepare Concrete Mix and Mount Panels to the Stand

Take cement and stones with 1:3 ratios and add water to make a thick mix. Pour concrete mix at each leg of the stand. Note that Debasiash made a heap-shaped concrete mix to give maximum strength. (One can secure it by using other methods. This example is for his specific situation.) As for mounting, the backsides of the solar panels have inbuilt holes for mounting. Match solar panel holes with the stand/platform holes and screw them together.

Wire the Solar Panel

At the back of the solar panel is a small junction box with positive and negative signs for polarity. In a large solar panel this junction box has terminal wires with a

MC4 connector; with small panels, you have to connect the junction box with external wires. Always try to use red and black wire for the positive and negative terminal connection. If there is provision for an earth wire, use a green wire for this.

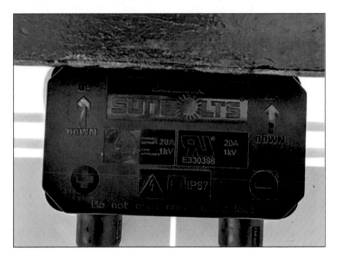

▲ The junction box.

Step 7: Series and Parallel Connection

After calculating the battery capacity and solar panel rating, you must now wire them. In many cases the calculated solar panel size or battery may not be available in the form of a single unit in the market. If you can't find the one you want, you have to add a small solar panel or batteries to match your system requirement. To match the required voltage and current rating we have to use series and parallel connections.

1. Series Connection: To wire any device in series you must connect the positive terminal of one device to the negative terminal of the next device.

SERIES CONNECTION

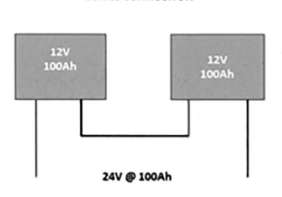

24V @ 100Ah

▲ The device in our case may be solar panel or battery. In series connection, the individual voltages of each device is additive.

Example: Let's say four 12V batteries are connected in series; then the combination will produce 12 + 12 + 12 + 12 = 48 volts. In series combination, the current or amperage is the same. So if these devices were batteries and each battery had a 12-volt rating and 100 Ah, then the total value of this series circuit is 48 Volts, 100Ah. If they were solar panels and each solar panel had a 17-volt rating (Osc voltage) and were rated at 5 amps each, then the total circuit value will be 68 volts, 5 amps.

2. Parallel Connection: In parallel connection you must connect the positive terminal of the first device to the positive terminal of the next device, and negative terminal of the first device to the negative terminal of the next device. In parallel connection the voltage remains the same but the current rating of the circuit is the sum of all the devices.

Example: Let's say two batteries of 12v, 100Ah are connected in parallel; then the system voltage remains 12 volts but the current rating is 100 + 100 = 200Ah. Similarly, if two solar panels of 17V and 5 amps are connected in parallel, then the system will produce 17 volts, 10 amps.

PARALLEL CONNECTION

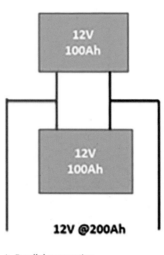

12V @200Ah

▲ Parallel connection.

Step 8: Inverter and Battery Stand

Debasiash Dutto made the inverter and battery stand above with the help of a carpenter. On the backside he made a big circular hole just behind the inverter fan for fresh air suction from the outside and later covered the hole with plastic wire mesh. A few small holes are also made for inserting the wires from the solar panel, charge controller, and inverter to the battery and AC output to the appliances. At both sides three horizontal holes are provided for sufficient ventilation. A glass window is provided at the front side to view the different led indications on the inverter. In the inclined plane of the inverter stand, Dutto mounted the charge controller. In the future he plans to install his own DIY energy meter.

Step 9: Wiring

▲ How to wire the system.

The first component we are going to wire is the charge controller. At the bottom of the charge controller are three signs. The first one from the left is for the connection of the solar panel having positive (+) and negative (-) signs. The second one with plus (+) and minus (-) signs is for the battery connection, and the last one is for the direct DC load connection, for such things as DC lights.

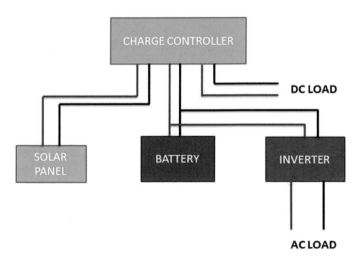

Always connect the charge controller to the battery first because this allows the charge controller to get calibrated to the system, be it 12V or 24V. Connect the red (+) and black (-) wire from the battery bank to the charge controller.

First connect the black/negative wire from the battery to the charge controller's negative terminal, and then connect the positive wire. After connecting the battery with the charge controller, you can see the charge controller indicator LED lights that indicate the battery level. After connecting this, inverter terminals for battery charging are connected to corresponding positive and negative terminals of the battery.

▲ Inverter AC output.

The next step is to connect the solar panel to the charge controller. On the back of the solar panel is a small junction box with two connected wires with positive (+) and negative (-) signs. The terminal wires are normally smaller in length.

To connect the wire to the charge controller, you need a special type of connector, commonly known as an MC4 connector. After connecting the solar panel to the charge controller, the green LED indicator will light up if sunlight is present.

Always connect the solar panel to the charge controller while facing the panel away from the sun or cover the panel with a dark material to avoid sudden high voltage coming from the solar panel to the charge controller, which may damage it.

Safety: It is important to note that we are dealing with DC current. The positive (+) is to be connected to positive (+) and negative (-) with negative (-) from solar panel to charge controller. If it gets mixed up, the equipment can break and may catch fire. So you need to be extremely careful when connecting these wires. It is recommended that you use two-color wires (i.e. red color for positive (+) and black color for negative (-). If you don't have red and black wire, wrap red and black tape at the terminals. Connect the DC load or DC light as the final step.

Additional Protection: Though the charge controller and inverter have inbuilt fuses for protection, you

▲ Solar panel.

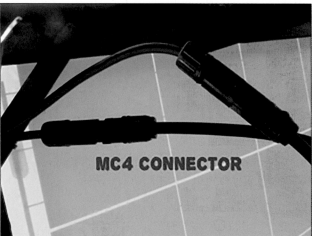

can put switches and fuses in the following places for additional protection and isolation.

1. In between solar panel and charge controller
2. In between charge controller and battery bank
3. In between battery and inverter

After wiring all components the off-grid solar system is ready for use.

Metering and Data Logging

If you're interested in knowing how much energy is produced by your solar panel or how much energy is being used, then you must use energy meters. You can also monitor your off-grid solar system by remote data logging.

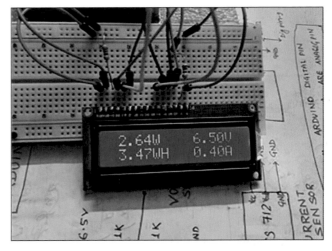

▲ Dutto's energy meter monitor.

Building a Water Wheel (Off-Grid in Australia)

Jill Redwood, an incredibly innovative woman, developed a power-generating water wheel for her off-grid home in East Gippsland, Australia, where she has lived alone, entirely off-grid with no power, water, mobile reception, or television, for over thirty years. Living on around $80 a week, Jill has more than sixty animals to keep her company and an abundant garden that serves as her grocery store right outside her kitchen door. Generating all her own (solar) power and collecting water from the local creek (via the water wheel shown below), Jill lives a life of her own creation. Here is how she does it:

Food: She grows a garden and developed a fruit orchard. Home-grown produce is her major food source. She provides her own dairy products as well; she has goats that provide milk and cheese and chickens for eggs. In fact, she is able to generate so much food that she sells some of her produce and eggs so she can get whatever small items she needs—mainly for her animals. She says she can go about six months without going into town—about an hour and a half away—for shopping items.

Photo courtesy of Jill Redwood

▲ Jill Redwood and her shepherd, Rafferty.

Photo courtesy of Jill Redwood

▲ Redwood tends to her garden.

Photo courtesy of Jill Redwood

▲ Redwood shares her harvest and supplements her income at the same time.

She supplements her cash flow by spotlighting her passion for the environment with her writing. But as you see, she doesn't just write about it, she lives the lifestyle that she promotes.

Shelter: Jill built her own house—a home that took eight years and $3,000 to build, during which time she lived in a small dirt-floored bark hut on the property. She had no homebuilding experience but had previously built shacks and chicken sheds, and had read about how early settlers used to build their homes. She said, "It's like baking a cake, you just follow the recipe." She filled the cracks in the timber walls (recycled timber off-cuts) of her home with a mixture of cow dung and lime in what she says is another early settlers' method for chinking up the holes in logs and awkward-to-get-to places.

I asked Jill if she could dig up the plans for her house when she was digging up the water wheel plan. "Plans for my house?" she asked. "That's ancient history, if I still even have it." She added, "The shire scratched their heads and didn't know what to do with it. Never seen any house plan like it before. But she just said to make every pole bigger. So now it'd be able to host a party of elephants."

Photo courtesy of Jill Redwood

▲ The "morning pick" from Redwood's harvest.

▲ Redwood framing the kitchen wall.

▲ The "cool room" in the finished kitchen.

▲ Two views of the exterior of the finished home.

▲ This is Redwood's "lounge" area.

▲ The all-important wood stove.

▲ Redwood's cook stove.

Power, Heating, and Cooking: "The power I use is minimal. I need the office equipment like the computer and scanner and the modem for the Internet," Jill explains. "I also use lights at night, a radio, and a food processor, and when the sun really shines and there's a lot of power coming in I've got a washing machine. That's a luxury." However, her main energy comes from her woodstove. It is her heat source, way to heat water, and to cook. Jill chops her own wood. "When I cook, it warms the house," she said. She goes on to say that it's just the basic old woodstove that people had used all the time for cooking. There is also a hot-water jacket in the firebox that thermo-syphons up to an insulated hot-water storage tank. She calls it "very common technology" and that it just requires "basic plumbing bits to join pipes and stuff." It also heats the house a bit but for colder winter nights she also has a wood heater; she claims it is a "Simple flu through the roof and standard fireproofing. No big deal."

Jill gathers all her own wood too. She said, "Getting wood is safer than going to town, and a chainsaw and ax are safer than a car on the road. You just have to know how to drive them properly." That makes sense to me when she puts it like that. She further "chastised" me by adding, "Seems strange that people would think that chopping wood is a marvelous achievement." Her woodstove is really old style (1930s), while the newer version (1950s) showcases some of its many uses to dry and warm and cook.

▲ Preserves: from the garden to the shelf.

▲ Installing solar panels. Redwood connected her own solar panels to generate electricity.

Photo courtesy of Jill Redwood

▲ Redwood cutting up firewood with her chainsaw.

Photo courtesy of Jill Redwood

▲ Pumpkin nets hang from the rafters.

Water Source: The Brodribb River—and her water wheel, described and pictured in detail below. It provides 1 liter/minute of water 24/7.

Plumbing: Zero. Her outhouse ("Dunny") is well equipped with a "toilet." And how has that been work-

ing out for thirty years? Perfectly. At times she adds ash on top of her "commode" with a bucket. And when it fills up? "You have to carry it out and bury it." Now that's leaving a tiny paw print.

Photo courtesy of Jill Redwood

▲ The "Dunny."

The Spiral Water Wheel: Jill told me the water wheel is the creation of a friend (John Hermans), who saw the basics in a kid's book—as a toy. She said, "He thought it could be sized up as a water wheel pump. I didn't build it. It's based on the Archimedes screw or something similar." Jill added, "John put it together in his workshop over a couple of weeks."

I asked Jill if she could supply me with the plans for the construction of the water wheel. She told me that she had them *somewhere*, if she could dig them up. And voila, almost no sooner were my words spoken (judging by the organization seen in her home's interior photos, she has everything at her fingertips!) than she had sent me an email back with the info, saying, "I actually wrote this up and put John's name on it as he was the brains behind it!" And to end this woman's incredible life journey; following is John Herman's article for the spiral water wheel for *Earth Garden* that Jill accommodatingly sent to me along with the plans (below) for the construction of the spiral water wheel itself.

Spiral Water Wheel, by John Hermans

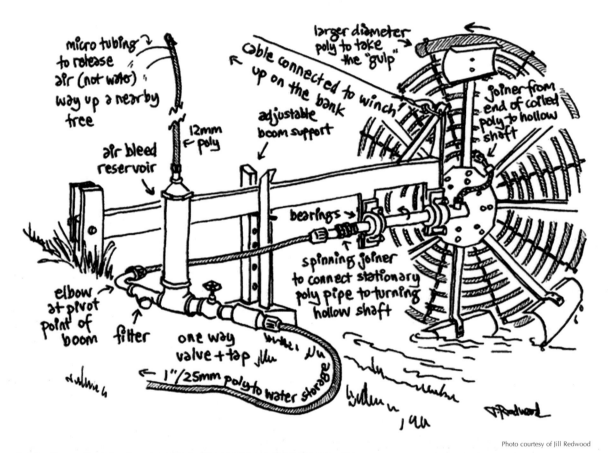

▲ John Hermans' spiral water wheel. Illustration courtesy *Earth Garden* magazine.

Low-impact lifestyler, John Hermans, devised and built a water wheel for Earth Garden*'s writer and forest campaigner Jill Redwood. It is silent, pumps about a litre a minute, goes twenty-four hours a day, has only one small moving part, and works on a very ancient principle.*

As I have no political lobbying or media skills, my way of helping the environment campaign is to help those committed to saving forests. My skills lie in the areas of inventing and building.

Jill had a 5HP fire-fighting pump she used to refill her concrete water tank each fortnight or so. I first devised an alternative pump using a set of water wheels which, via chains and cogs that gave a 4:1 step up, drove a small piston pump.

The petrol pump was temperamental and noisy. This improved model was temperamental and oily. It did work quite well but was prone to occasional mechanical failure and there was the possibility of it leaking oil into the pristine Brodribb River. So I got to work on an idea I had seen illustrated as a kids' toy. As Jill lives on the upper reaches of the Brodribb River, the small flow in the river was not enough to operate a ram pump. The spiral water wheel has the benefit of being environmentally friendly, all but maintenance free, made of basic cheap materials, and is relatively easy to make for anyone with a welder.

This positive displacement pump is made from a single length of coiled polypipe and is designed to be powered by water. The pipe is coiled in a vertical plane and mounted on a horizontal axle. As the paddles rotate the coil of polypipe above the water, the lower part is immersed. The open end of the coil takes a small 'gulp' of water every time it rotates. An alternating sequence of air and water is driven along the pipe towards the center of the spiral. Successive coils of pipe lead to a cumulative increase in the pump's pressure output. When a land-fixed pipe is connected to the last and smallest coil, then water can be shifted to a higher point, such as a dam or a tank. (Note: In this case, Jill has a tank that is about sixteen meters above the river.)

The set of undershot paddle wheels (powered from water flowing below, not from water dropping onto the wheels from above—or overshot wheel) drives the whole show. This is one of the oldest and simplest forms of motor, driving one of the oldest and simplest forms of pump. The whole unit consists of just one small rotating part called a rotating joiner, or in plumber terms a spinning nipple.

When assembling the coils on the spokes of the frame, I had no idea how many coils and at what diameter was needed to pump the water to the sixteen-meter head. The water wheel ended up about two meters in diameter. As the water wheel and the spiral both needed to dip into the water, the coil has to be the same diameter as the paddles.

Three-quarter-inch polypipe can be coiled down to about 500mm in diameter before it starts to kink. If the coils are kept close together, around forty coils can be made. I decided to make two lots of coils consisting of twenty coils each, so there were two openings to take a gulp. In theory this should have pumped twice the volume of water as a single coil rotating at the same speed. However, this proved to be too heavy for the flow of the stream to move, so I had to take one coil of pipe out. As Jill's place is three hours drive away, there was much guesswork involved in my workshop and redesigning on site.

The final coil design saw fifty meters of three-quarter-inch (18 mm) polypipe coiled into twenty loops from two meters to half a meter diameter. The pumping rate at this site is about one liter a minute but varies season to season.

My theory then is that to successfully pump water, the coiled pipe needs to be about three times as long as the height it is being pumped to. That's a 3:1 ratio. I assume that the size of the pipe is less important than the total length. Larger loops are more effective at forcing water up than small loops but consume more length. Fewer larger loops may be just as effective as many smaller loops.

The water exiting the smallest coil in the center is piped into the hollow shaft of the water wheel's axle. The end of this then joins a stationary water pipe near the bank, in this case connected to a boom arm (described below). To join the rotating shaft to the fixed polypipe, a joiner is needed that can spin constantly. Unless the connection is perfectly in line, these watertight rotating joiners can wear out quickly.

To avoid flood damage to this water wheel pump, I mounted the axle and bearings onto a three-meter boom of 100mm RHS that pivots at the end anchored to the bank. Along this boom, a height-adjustable support is set into the bank. A steel cable is attached to the water wheel that is operated by a winch fixed even higher up the bank. (See the illustration and the photo with Jill on the bank.) Not only does this allow it to be cranked out of the water if a flood is imminent and hoisted safely above flood height, but it also allows the water wheel to be lowered or raised to match the high and low river flows.

Photo courtesy of Jill Redwood

Photo courtesy of Jill Redwood

Here are a few more pointers to help with constructing the coil section. To attach the polypipe to the angle iron spokes, use 1mm stainless-steel wire (order from engineering suppliers). The end of the three-quarter-inch polypipe that scoops up the water should be increased in diameter for the last loop. I used one inch for half a loop and then one and a quarter inch polypipe for the last half a loop. This allows for greater volume to be scooped up each rotation. As both water and air are pumped up the delivery line together, it is best to send the pumped water directly to the storage tank or dam. If the inlet and outlet line to the tank is the same, a special air bleed line close to the pump will be needed, as Jill discovered when trying to use the taps on the same line or have a shower!

A one-way valve will also need to be set in the line to stop water draining back out when the wheel is not pumping. A filter isn't a bad idea either. You can also fix a fly wire guard to the inlet end of the coil that reduces debris from entering the system.

One modification that had to be made over the last couple of years has been a more robust and reinforced hollow shaft. The constant flexing and movement of the water wheel, especially with faster flows, stresses metal and any weak spots are soon discovered.

The water wheel was sited on a slight bend in the river where it was narrow and the water had a higher velocity.

Variables that allow this design to pump effectively are:

- River flow
- Size of paddles
- Number of paddles
- Diameter of the wheel
- Diameter and number of the coils
- Submergence of the coils
- Inlet pipe diameter
- Height of storage tank/dam.

Note: This spiral pump was a direct replacement of a small standard piston pump and has proved to be just as efficient at pumping a set volume per day. Overall, it's a beautiful piece of alternate technology.

Photo courtesy of Jill Redwood

8. Maintenance and Special Considerations

Once the cabin was restored and everything was perfect, Gary turned to me one warm afternoon as we sat on our deck, he with a beer in hand and I with my ever-present coffee cup in mine, and asked me the loaded question: "Are we done yet?" He was referring to our cabin renovation and all the ongoing details along with it, which I have fully described. I smiled. Of course the answer is "No." As we all know, one is never really done with a cabin project, is one? The same is true for home projects as well. Why? Because there is always upkeep involved along with special considerations to keep the cabin safe and secure when you are away. And we thought we would "get away from it all" at the cabin. But there is a difference between cabin and home projects: it is *fun* to do these things at the cabin.

Securing the Cabin Between Visits

Let's start with securing the cabin between visits. After a few times, this short list of to-dos becomes ingrained in you.

- First, I thoroughly clean the cabin and air it out if necessary to mitigate food and cooking smells that may tempt a bear to investigate. I bring out the kitchen garbage and combine it with the garbage already collected in a large bag/s in the basement, which we stored during our visit. (I never include food items or anything with food smells downstairs in that garbage until the day we are leaving.) We couldn't bear the thought of a big bear rummaging in our basement and wreaking havoc in the middle of the night. They are very curious animals and their nose is directly connected to their stomach. Did I mention that they are also huge? They are not to be messed with up close, or even at a distance, as they are deceptively fast on their feet. And they do not like their snack time interrupted. We always bring all garbage back with us.
- Once done using the water, Gary goes downstairs to the basement and turns off the PEX line valves for both the hot and cold water. Then he drains the water from both water lines into two buckets, one for each line. In summer we wouldn't need to

do this as the pipes will not freeze, of course, but he made the shutoff process so easy he just does it at the same time. This is a necessary step if we are winterizing the cabin during the snowy period when we know we won't be able to get to it for a while.

- Once the water is drained from below, I turn on the hot and cold water taps in the kitchen, bathroom sink, and shower. We also learned the hard way to squeeze out the water from the kitchen spray nozzle, as we returned on one occasion to find the hose broken due to freeze damage. In addition, this also helps in the final water drainage and ensures that air is not trapped in pipes and mitigates cavitation when you turn water back on.
- Gary puts Rid-X down the toilet once a month or more often at the time we leave the cabin as well. The microbes in this powder break down solids in your septic tank. We did not change the original three-hundred-gallon septic tank, but we did install a new six-inch drain hose from the cabin downhill to the septic system. A good leach line system was also already in place. The septic tank was covered by a heavy piece of metal at all times. However, sometimes Gary would have to go down the hill and recover it if a bear pawed it away.
- If we visit the cabin in colder weather, we also always pour the "pink stuff," as I called it down the toilet shower and sink drains after the water was drained off. The pink stuff is actually antifreeze for household use. And the purpose is to protect the pipes from damage or freezing.
- The Champion generator is also secured. Though Gary insists on using aviator gas because it will not plug the generator and runs clean, he still drains the carburetor: With the generator running, he simply turns the fuel valve on/off switch to off and it just runs until the fuel is drained from the carburetor and sputters to a stop. When we arrive back to the cabin, he turns the fuel switch back to on. It is just an extra maintenance precaution and so simple to do.
- If it is summertime, we check beforehand to make sure every sprinkler in the irrigation drip system

and the lawn rain bird sprinkler (operated by timers) are both working properly. Gary changes the batteries in the timers every spring and always keeps a couple of new timers and lots of drip system parts on hand in the basement.

- He also takes the Honda up to the 3000-gallon tank to make sure nothing has been damaged or is leaking. Then he rides up a quarter mile farther to the road where we installed the two-inch PVC line (replacing the aluminum irrigation pipe) and installed the new steel spring box in order to clean out the filter and do a quick check of the line for damage from falling rocks, trees, or bears. He first unlocks the padlock on the steel box lid and swings it back. Keeping it locked stops curious two-legged predators from opening it and messing around with the rather fragile filter system. *(Note: More often than not these maintenance tasks are done upon our arrival, especially if water in the little fountain is not spraying strongly upward as it normally does or if the little lake below the cabin seems low.)* Again, in this case Gary keeps a large inventory of special fittings and parts to repair damage. We do not want to be without our precious water, even if we have a 3000-gallon reservoir. To date, he's only needed to make one minor repair to a leaking connection.

- What is the very last thing we do before we leave? We double-check all doors to the main cabin, the basement, and the little cabins, to make sure they are locked. The basement, shower house, and two small cabin doors are padlocked.

Maintenance

- Just when I thought I could put the rake down after all my rock raking in our compound, I was proven wrong. I had not taken into consideration the leaves, nor the accumulation of pine needles. For fire protection, it is a must to rake them up before fire season hits and clear off the area by eliminating this fuel supply to fires. We would rake the needles, pine cones, and leaves into piles and burn them in the fall before it got too wet, or in early spring. We eventually found that we could rake them onto a large tarp tied to the Honda and drag many large piles quickly far on down the road; spilling the tarp over a distant cliffside ,out of harm's way. That way we could clean up some heavy duty piles in short order, without the worry of timing the burning or watching the burnng piles.

- Gary also at times takes our leaf blower up on the roof to remove the needles from the metal and around the stovepipe on our cabin and on lower cabin.

- We never, ever come up to the cabin without at least one chainsaw; ideally, Gary carries two along with saw tools and chainsaw gas. Why? We never know when we'll find a tree lying across the road. If we go up after a big storm we hold our breath until we go through both gates and eventually park at our cabin. Our hearts sink if we round a turn to see a fallen tree across the road, waiting for Gary to cut up. It's not always fun, especially as we are always anxious to get to the cabin. But after a few minutes, as I throw the brush off to the side of the road amid the buzz of Gary's chainsaw, it actually can be fun. Then we stack the wood along the roadside for later pick up, because of course it meant firewood for our Lopi woodstove. It's always nice to have a wood supply on hand, though at times we supplement the wood by bringing a trailer load from our house so we can burn fires with giddy abandon without thought to the wood usage. A fire is so nice to sit in front of! And the three of us (Greta too, of course) often build a fire outside in our iron fire pit/BBQ, often cooking our dinner on the grate we fabricated to fit our huge iron scalding pot. After the fire burns down, Gary puts the large metal lid he had made at the same time back over the top both as protection against flying sparks and to shield it from taking on water from the lawn sprinkler set to come on in the summer every day at 6 a.m. In addition, we discovered other great fire starters that are in constant supply and easy to access. We go on Honda ride scavenger hunts with Greta to collect the plentiful extra-large sugar pine cones, full of pitch. (We use gloves.) I also keep many of the smaller ones I rake up around the cabin for the same purpose. We store them in a large wine barrel alongside the wood-pile kept under the deck.

- Other chainsaw work includes pruning the fruit trees in the fall. Gary does some manually with his nineteen-foot pole saw, like the ones he'd used for years pruning in our walnut orchards. Periodically, he also uses the gas-powered pole saw I bought him several years ago for Father's Day. The gas-powered saw also comes in handy when he touches up the regrowth of Manzanita and overhead tree branches along the one-mile-plus roadway entrance to the cabin. As I've mentioned, it was quite an undertaking to initially cut the trees and Manzanita overgrowth back from the roadway. Gary wants to keep it in hand with minimal effort, so he takes the Honda down the road cutting on one side as he goes, and the other on the way back whenever he feels it needs a touch up. Manzanita is resilient and fast growing.

- Though we have not had to do too much outdoor maintenance, some deck and cabin paint upkeep is necessary. After all, we do live in the real world even if the cabin and surrounding area is like a fairyland.

- Originally, we stained the deck with a high quality stain that our contractor, Steve Downey, recommended. Initially, however, the Doug-fir wood was not completely dry—in fact, it was still rather green— and oozed pitch in some places. After a couple years we needed to pressure wash the deck and roll on the same extremely expensive stain again. All things considered, though, the stain didn't hold up that great to the snow and sun, in spite of its price tag. So after several more years we brought the pressure washer up again in our little trailer hauler and washed it all again. This time, though, we switched to Kelly Moore brand paint our cabin painter Kirk recommended. We bought it in a chocolate color that was lighter than our cabin, in order to add contrast. It was a very warm day when we took the task on. We rolled on

▶ Interior of the original roof, which was falling in. Gary shored it up, then installed an old window that we found in the basement.

the paint with special long-handled rollers after I cut in all the edges against the cabin and shower house. And this time, unlike the last, we did all the slats in the railing and all the upper and lower deck beams. It was a lot of work, but it looked fabulous when we were done. And the paint just glued itself onto the boards in one thick, luscious coat. And we think it looks better and richer than the stain. It's been foolproof since, delivering against rain, sun, and snow.

- As for the cabin itself, we have only had to do some light touch up on the original cedar of the lower boards of the basement, where the dirt splashes up during periods of heavy rainfall. Kirk sprayed the same high-quality Kelly Moore paint in the Java color on our cabin exterior, the shower house, and the two small cabins. It simply rejuvenated the old wood and protected it against further decay and damage. I touch up the base around these cabins periodically, due again to the mud splash-up from rain. However, having used Hardie Board on the entire cabin during the

remodel process, as I discussed above its resistance to all kinds of weather and snow damage is remarkable. It looks untouched—like concrete. (Well, come to think of it, it is made of cement, sand, and cellulose fibers.) And believe me, I check it out regularly with my paintbrush always ready. I cannot recommend the Hardie Board or Kelly Moore paint enough. They don't sell Kelly Moore at Home Depot, at least not in our area. Don't compromise.

- We also installed and maintain special smoke, gas, and CO2 detectors (about $60 each), changing the nine-volt batteries every year in the spring. We took this extra precaution against gas leakage because of our 1920 propane-powered Servel refrigerator (though vented to the outdoors) and our 1950 O'Keefe and Merritt vintage stove.

- We also installed a special triple-walled eight-inch DuraPlus Stove chimney pipe that is extra safe; the pipe is cool to the touch when the fire is burning HOT. Of course, we tiled both under and around the woodstove for added protection.

◀ Our fire pit, with lid and grate in the background. Originally, this antique was used as a scalding pot to soak pigs in, so that the bristles can be easily scraped off before the pig is processed and cooked.

- For fire protection outside the cabin, Gary also installed roof sprinklers in case of fire threat. I have discussed the four fire hydrants above, two of which were tie-ins (linked to the 3000-gallon water tank water supply above the cabin) and six hundred feet of fire hose. He regularly checks the valves, which are all protected in ten-inch-diameter PVC housing covered by a large PVC cap.

Heating and Cooling

- Heating and cooling considerations are simple, few, and effective. To heat the cabin, we use the small but efficient Lopi woodstove. The cabin was never insulated and we did not plan to do so, as we didn't plan to spend long periods of time there during winter. The wood usage was minimal, supplemented by pinecones for starter fuel. This was no doubt due in part to the small size it needed to heat and the low ceiling in the main living area, though some of the heat did rise to the upstairs loft where we could sit and read. It gets quite toasty there. We considered bringing up a small space heater for the bedroom at night but never found it necessary. On particularly cold nights, Gary at times puts an extra chunk or two on the fire to keep it going with hot coals for the morning.
- We have no a/c nor do we feel the need for it. Though we are in the mountains and at 4100 feet, the temperatures do climb into the triple digits. The upside? There is almost always a breeze, and at night it cools down dramatically. What is the answer when the sun sparkles and shines? A cold beer on the shady deck, of course! But what about Greta's remedy? She lies on the grass under the tree, sometimes with a fresh dog bone straight from the freezer. She alternates that spot with her little cool dirt "nest cave" that she climbs into under the porch. But of course those are not the only ways we keep cool, or I'd have to keep the Budweiser Clydesdales and their fully stocked beer wagon on standby at the cabin. For cooling we designed the windows and sliding door placement to take advantage of passive energy, relying on the breezes that often blew to cool the entire

area. Before it would warm up too much, around midmorning, we opened the door in the loft and latched the screen door closed. That way all the rising heat escaped outside. The overhang we added to the front entrance helps immensely, with shading keeping the main living room cool. We often leave the front door open when we are in the cabin or on the deck. In the late afternoon we draw the special light-reducing drapes in the bedroom closed across the three windows, as the sun beats into that room. It is very effective in dropping the temperature there up to 20°F. We did test a battery-powered compact fan with a water reservoir, but sent the $99 European-made unit back on the same slow boat it arrived on. Return shipping was astronomical. It was advertised to cool an entire room in minutes, but had no air output and was not frosty or even *cool*. Not even close. Lesson learned. If what you have works, don't try to fix it or improve it.

Security Considerations

- A rancher friend of ours once told us that good fences make good neighbors. The same is true with a good gate. And we have three, all with padlocks on them. As I mentioned, two of the gates are on the roadway going into our cabin. The first one, one and a half miles from the cabin, is shared with our great neighbors Dan and Robin. Their cabin lies to the left down a ravine roughly a mile along our roadway into the property. So that gate is a security measure for their cabin as well as ours. Our gate (the second gate) is a half-mile farther, where the water from the spring area cascades down almost like a waterfall, running under the road at the left of our gateway out of a large culvert. It is always a welcome sight and sound as I climb out to unlock the gate before we drive past it on the final leg up the hill, past the craggy "mountain lion rock" to our cozy abode. Gate No. 3 is far above the cabin on our property. It is a dirt road that hunters from all over use during hunting season, and allowed them access to our (private) road and (private) property. There's a name for that. It's called trespassing. The previous owner, Bard, let Gary know he'd had a heck of a time with trespassers. (When he sold us the cabin, he was eighty-five years old and as honest as the day was long.) Of course all that changed when Gary came to town. He installed a twelve-foot steel gate in a spot where both the uphill and downhill sides of the road were much too tight and steep to maneuver a vehicle or ATV around. He built in a six-inch concrete post on the swing side of the gate and anchored the hinge side to a twelve-inch yellow pine. The finishing touch was the jewelry: the heavy-duty steel chain double-wrapped (not cuttable with a bolt cutter) around the gate and post and secured with a heavy duty "locket." It had a key to open it. Very romantic.

- I cannot say enough about the value of good neighbors, as I mentioned earlier, as it offers a bonus to your security and peace of mind almost better than a security camera. We look after each other. It is a brotherhood and sisterhood that we share on the mountain. It is comforting to have someone watching your back—someone you can trust, someone you don't have to ask to give you a hand, someone who expects nothing in return, someone you want to have putting their feet under your dinner table. We are lucky. But it is not a given. You must prove yourself, and I don't mean by offering out a beer around the campfire. In order to have a good friend, you have to be one.

- Speaking of security cameras, we put up Moultrie trail cameras at strategic locations all over our property. How do you think "Mountain Lion Rock" got its name? Field cameras are relatively inexpensive ($99-$150, with an additional $30 for the memory chip for photos). They are great recording tools for not only monitoring four-legged intruders, but the two-legged ones as well. Gary mounts them on their metal bracket to a tree or post such as on our deck. He checks them upon each visit and changes locales as he deems it necessary. He has the option after viewing photos of erasing them or removing the chip to take in (to CVS, for example) to print. He turns the one positioned on our deck off upon our arrival, and then back on just before we leave. It is not uncommon to find a large bear on the camera, looking into and nosing up our living room window. He also gets up into Gary's and my two-seated wooden chair that we refurbished (circa 1950s—it was at the cabin) to look in, leaving his footprints behind. We marvel that he doesn't break it. It just proves they don't build things like they used to.

Dealing With Animal Damage

- **Mice**. Let me start with the small critter control: mice and/or rats. They are small but can cause incredible damage to electrical wiring, not to mention the poop and pee they leave behind. As I described in our cabin cleanup/cleanout process, an out-of-control mice or rat infestation can cause incredible damage—and I believe is a health risk when you have to breathe in that atmosphere. We use mice/rat poison "bricks' called "Tomcats," which we buy in little buckets. We also use the warfarin pellets in trays that you can buy in boxes. We put it in our cabin basement, inside the Pelton wheel cabin, and in the lower cabin too. When we renovated the cabin, Gary and I couldn't help but remember the unforgettable mice mess we had to clean up. Not wanting a repeat, he asked Steve Downey to fill every hole and crevice with whatever was necessary to eliminate the problem. We have not had one single mouse sign in the cabin since. Gary also sealed all the holes and cracks in the lower cabin with caulking, while I worked on the inside, filled the gaping crack all around the little cabin roofline between the walls and tin roof using one-inch-wide rolls of insulation. I stuffed it in tightly and followed up by covering it over with a six-inch-wide roll of fine mesh that I stapled in place. While not completely foolproof, that in combination with the poison worked wonders to control the problem. While I see some sign at times, I have never seen a live mouse (or a dead one) in the two small cabins.

- **Bears**. On the other hand, warfarin does not get rid of the plentiful black bears in our area. How do we know? Well, one tore out the side of our Pelton wheel cabin, staggered around inside the small building, and ate thirteen WHOLE boxes (not individual trays) of warfarin that Gary had stored there. We thought that was the end of him, so we replaced all the cedar boards on the side of the cabin and I repainted them. But that was not the end of the story. A week later, while we were gone, he came back and tore out the *other* side of the cabin, looking for more. I know bears love peanut butter, bacon, and popcorn—we even heard a story about a bear that broke in twice to the same cabin, opened the freezer, and ate ice cream—but warfarin?

▲ A local black bear. Credit: Getty Images

The solution is simple. Keep everything clean and odor free, mainly when you depart. That includes no BBQ residue or smell on our fire pit grate. Leave NO garbage behind, like I already mentioned. We also put two heavy-duty screen doors on opposite sides of our back porch inside of which is a heavy-duty latched cabinet (built by a friend in his woodshop) where we keep our six to eight screw-on-lid five-gallon buckets that con-

tain flour and such along with other non-foodstuff sundry items. The only invasion was a bear cub that left his claw mark down the screen before he carefully pried back the bottom half of extra heavy screen and squeezed in. We saw his muddy little paw prints as proof. He did no damage whatsoever and left the same way he got in. Gary did not replace the door but wired the screen shut again and left the claw marks as a conversation piece—and for posterity.

I also try not to cook bacon or fish at the cabin, or at least not for a day or two before we leave. Of course I air everything out as I am cleaning.

We considered many suggestions offered to keep the bears at bay. We decided not to do any of them. Among them were bars on the windows, or boarding up windows and doors every time we left, then removing them on arrival. What a chore! Another was laying nail-spiked boards in front of windows and doors.

- **Ants, Spiders, Wasps, and Bees.** Though we don't have much problem with ants or spiders, we found a great spray product at Home Depot to stop them in their tracks. It is called "Hot Shot" and works on ants, roaches, and spiders. Gary would spray it directly on and around ants and on any webs that appeared. (Before I can sweep them down!) As for wasps and bees, they were only particulary pesky at meal times. In order to mitigate this problem we bought the yellow plastic canister traps, again found at Home Depot. And we hang them up near where we eat or grill outdoors. Gary found that small chunks of meat or chicken were most effective as bait. However, he also used the bait that can be bought with the traps and it worked too.

- **Mountain Lions.** How in the world do you stop a mountain lion encounter, if one happens, from turning ugly? We have never seen one live, only on the field cameras. But we are always aware they are there. Gary's friend since childhood became a game warden. He once told Gary to be careful on the ranch where we live and to carry a gun. Gary said jokingly that I carry a walking stick and I will club it and chase it off. He said you won't even see it coming. It will attack from behind and lock its jaws around your neck. Gary never forgot that. For that reason *I never walk alone at the cabin*, and I carry a walking stick and a gun on my hip.

Credit: Getty Images

▲ Mountain lions are in the area; we always keep a lookout.

Greta is always with us and she alerts to any creature, even a lizard or a squirrel, before we know it is there. However, that never stops us from taking long walks, though we don't do so at dusk. And when we pass Mountain Lion Rock, I always cautiously look it over, anticipating the possibility of spotting a crouched lion waiting to pounce from above.

Protecting the Fruit Trees

- Forget it. You just cannot protect your orchard completely from the bears or deer. They love apples, peaches, and apricots. We know. We have seen the baby cubs on the field cameras scoot up the trees and knock apples down to their waiting mamas below. It is cute, but so frustrating. The deer eat their share as well, and strip all the leaves off the lower branches or devastate our newly planted young trees. I can't count the number of times we have replanted the trees hoping to get them to the point where they will be big enough to weather the havoc.

- One morning I awoke at 6 a.m. and looked out the window up into the orchard as I always do. I did a double take. Sitting on his haunches twenty feet from the window was a huge (five-hundred-pounds plus, Gary estimated) old bear. He was so fat he could not be troubled to move. I saw he was already panting from the warmth of the early morning and, as I gazed in wonder, he simply reached up with one giant arm and pulled a huge limb down to him and began eating the apples. Gary and I both watched silently as he crunched away, then slowly got up with great effort and waddled silently back into the woods. Even Greta watched quietly from the bed, awestruck. (We had whispered to her, "*Not a sound*!!")

- One well-meaning acquaintance suggested hanging small fruit jars filled with mothballs in the trees to ward off bears and deer. Eyes watering, I painstakingly filled each tiny jar, put the lid on, and wrapped wire around the mouth, leaving enough wire so I could hang it from the tree. When I was done, Gary poked holes in the lids. The effort was ground into the dirt—literally, as we found the jars scattered over the orchard or hanging precariously still in the trees, the acrid ammonia smell totally ignored by the marauding bears. While the deer used more delicate methods, nibbling the tender shoots of the smaller trees—either over, around, or through the staked-out and wire-wrapped circle, they were no less destructive. The good news is that Greta was always on guard duty when we were at the cabin. She chased the bears and the deer back into the woods or some distance beyond, over to our dear neighbor Bill Haase's cabin. He has forty huge, vintage apple trees that are attacked regularly by bears.

- It is as though Mother Nature is mocking us. My suggestion then? Go with the flow. Do what you can to grow your orchard, roses, or lawn, but don't allow your frustrations to tarnish the real reason you are there. Tritely put, that reason is to commune with nature, not fight against it. If you want to shoot something, wait until a Timber Rattler crosses your path. Lead poisoning is the most effective extermination method against these dangerous snakes and the only thing they seem to understand. And they blend in so well with their surroundings. Gary is always telling me to watch my step! With good reason. Is it any wonder I never venture forth without my Colt strapped on and latched down? My gun belt is always full of bullets too.

9. Securing Your Investment with an Insurance Policy

I am writing this final chapter as an addendum to my book just before it goes to press. I am doing so not only because my editor suggested I do so, but also because after some thought, I feel it is so important. I want to *strongly* advise making sure your cabin has an excellent insurance policy, just as you do with your home and vehicle. If possible, make it a policy that covers your treasure in all instances and for every scenario, including vandalism, water damage, storm damage, fallen trees, and fire. Let me explain.

I described earlier the National Forest Service lookout above our cabin. It is located at 7000 feet in the Shasta Trinity National Forest. Until recently it was manned (or womaned) by Rachel. What a godsend and asset she was to have on hand. It was such a comfort to know that she was, from her magnificent vantage point, watching for any hint of fire that she could spot within a one hundred mile, 360-degree radius. She told us that if we were at the cabin in the event of a wildfire and could not escape by any other means, we were to drive up to her at the lookout and she would have us airlifted to safety.

Unfortunately, that protection left us when Rachel retired in 2018 after thirty-plus years. She had worked twenty-four-hour live-in-the-lookout shifts five days a week all during fire season, with someone filling in for her two days a week. She was a wealth of

▲ The circular "map" that Rachel uses to spot and pinpoint area of a fire.

knowledge on the terrain, wildlife, and geology of the area. The beautiful, historic lookout tower was eventually closed after she retired, and soon fell into disrepair. In the following fire seasons of 2019 and 2020 we in California were suffering from a severe draught and, as Gary said, everything was drier than a popcorn ball. Never were Rachel and the lookout needed more.

The lightning strikes in 2019 came close to our cabin and smoke from surrounding forest fires turned the blue mountain sky to gray all summer. Gary made countless phone calls to NFS headquarters and could actually monitor the entire vista of "Tom Head Mountain" from our home's porch. He was the lookout man, as all our cabin neighbors called on him as he monitored the progress of the fire's path. It was excruciating. He coordinated efforts with the NFS fire control team and told them the lay of the land and urged them to start dumping retardant on the fire by air, as the terrain was too steep to fight on the ground. When authorized to do so, he drove to the staging area near the cabin, brought maps, and talked to the fire crew and captains who had traveled from all over the United States; walked the trails and showed one of the captains from Idaho the roads he had built on our property all the way up to the lookout that would allow for equipment and crew access. The ash covered our deck like snow.

While Gary was up at the cabin, I stayed home on the ranch with Greta. I could hear the rumbling of the bombers, and I watched them one after the other fly over our home on their way to the mountain forty miles distant as the crow flies. It was comforting to know that with each drop, our cabin and all our neighbors' cabins were one step closer to being out of danger from fire. After weeks of worry and fear that the wind would change direction, we finally breathed a sigh of relief.

In 2020, the drama continued. In mid-July, Gary and I got up in the wee hours of the morning, watching a thunder and lightning storm like none other. It was a true phenomenon. It lasted for hours, lighting up the sky all around us. It was magnificent. We heard later there were over four thousand strikes in the state, including one on our ranch that took hold the next day and was quickly put out by CALFIRE and Rancho Tehama Fire Department, as someone in "Rancho Tehama Reserve" three miles away across the creek from our ranch thankfully reported it. They were able to stop it after only a few acres of burn. We wouldn't even have known about it as the trucks came in through the back of our ranch. But one of the trucks, upon leaving the site, lost its way and ended up at midnight at our compound gate. We were astounded. Their red lights were flashing and it was quite a spectacle. We didn't even know what kind of a vehicle it was at first. Our ranch is in the middle of nowhere. The fire crew still at the site that night told Gary (after he raced over to check it out) that the fire was stopped after only a few acres had burned, due largely to one of the fire breaks Gary had made that spring with his tractor and float. It had burned to the break and thankfully stopped. The two captains there told him that basically they only had to mop up.

We thought that was it. And yet again we felt a tremendous relief. Little did we imagine the carnage that was yet to follow. California was again in the national spotlight for the second year in a row, the headlines screaming "All Of California Is On Fire." That was no understatement. A couple days later we drove up to our cabin to spend several days. There was not a hint of smoke anywhere around and the sky was dazzling blue. It was so remarkably clear and bright. We settled in as we always do. The next morning we awoke and went about our usual routine, though we noticed smoke from a fire in the distance far to the south of us across the valley. We assumed it was far away and would be quickly snuffed. But this year it was different. Fires were burning all over the state—and all at once. California was short staffed in our area because crews were being sent to other parts of the state. The regular crews, trucks, and heavy equipment and bombers were not available. What was left was spread too thin.

Before we knew what was happening, our son Andrew was calling on his cell. He said "You gotta get out of there, I just saw in a news alert on my phone that they are closing the road to the mountain." He told us that no one could get in and that everyone on the mountain and far below us into the valley was being ordered to evacuate. Gary called over to Bill Haase immediately, as he was at his cabin as well. We packed up quickly, loaded Greta into the Suburban, and headed down to the airport landing two miles down the road from our cabin, where we met up with Bill and began to convoy down the mountain. As we drove the steep ridge road, spotter planes roared overhead. Smoke was everywhere. Soon the bombers followed and we had front-row seats as they dropped retardant several hundred yards south of us. The fire had jumped Cottonwood Creek and was heading north toward us and continued to burn north, then west as well as the wind changed. We finally made it home. Over the next several days, all we could do was wait. Gary kept watch from our porch, using his high-powered binoculars. The smoke was engulfing the mountain and it was hard to see where the fire was actually burning, but it was oh so close to our cabin, we could see that for sure.

The next evening we took a picnic dinner up to "our hill" on the ranch, where over thirty years prior Gary

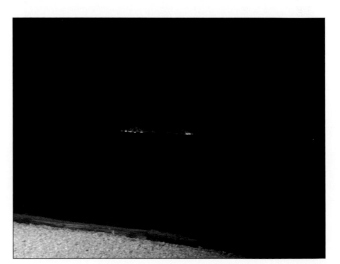

▲ From our ranch, we could see the fire burning on our mountain forty miles away. All we could do was wait.

had asked me to marry him. From that 1000-foot, almost-360-degree panoramic vantage point (the highest peak on the ranch), we could see the fires burning in the foothills and along *every* ridgeline. Tom Head Mountain was illuminated as though it were a volcano. It was something one would have to see and experience firsthand to believe. And it is nothing I want to ever see again. We had no news reports on our cabin. Three long days went by.

On a Friday morning, Bill Haase called. He was able to get up to his cabin with his son and reported that his cabin had been spared so far, but that the fire was burning all around him and was right up to his gate. He, his son, and a few friends had already begun to build a perimeter around his cabin, using his D-5 Cat and other equipment. CAL FIRE brought a hand crew in to help. Bill stayed for several weeks, at the mercy of the winds, battling to save it. He did.

Though still burning in his area, the fire had pretty much swept through our side of the mountain. Bill's son managed to make it over to our place to check to see if it was okay. I remember the call vividly. I'd come out onto the porch where Gary had taken the call. And Bill said, "Dwayne made it over to your cabin, Gary. Burned trees had fallen across the road but he walked the rest of the way." Gary said, "Was everything okay?" Bill hesitated. And we knew. He said, "It's gone Gary. All gone. I am so sorry." We were stunned. I could see it in Gary's face as well. It must have mirrored my own. But I have to hand it to him; he kept his composure and continued to speak at length with Bill.

I quietly went inside, pulling the screen door shut. Then I pulled the heavy cabin photo album down out of the cabinet and started flipping through it. Not that it did much good because I could barely make out the blur of images, ones I had grown to know by heart. I was sobbing. (And I never sob, or even cry much.) Greta, who was always on alert, knew something was awry and snuffled and nudged at my knee.

Finally, Gary came in and told me he wanted to go up to the cabin, and he wanted to go this morning. I said how is that possible? Will they allow vehicles through? He said he wasn't taking NO for an answer from anyone. He was going. Besides, Bill was at his

▲ When we got to the site, there was a small fire still burning.

cabin. He looked at me and said, "You don't have to go." I just looked back at him and wondered from where he drew his strength. I didn't think I *could* go. As waves of pain washed over me, I said to myself, it was too soon! I wasn't ready. In fact I may *never* be ready. Then I went.

Gary shared more news on the drive to the cabin. I thought Dan and Robin's cabin also had to be gone. But he had learned from Bill (as his son Dwayne had to go right by it on the way to our place) that miraculously it had been spared. Gary called Dan to let him know before we left the house. We checked it out for Dan on the way in so Gary could report more back to him after our trip. Though his water lines had been melted and would need replacing, the cabin had been left completely untouched, including the freshly stained wooden deck. I marveled; How is this possible? Down

▲ The 3000-gallon tank, melted flat as a pancake.

▲ View to the lower cabin site.

in a densely wooded ravine? It was incomprehensible. Without an ounce of intervention, the fire had swept by within feet of the cabin *on both sides*. But our cabin, one-quarter mile distant, had been completely consumed. Everything was burned to the ground; in fact, the fire was still burning a bit on the cabin debris. The new propane tank, its once dazzling white surface now slightly charred, was hissing ominously. The shower house, the Pelton wheel cabin, and the lower cabin, along with every bit of our entire water system, were disintegrated. The pond was dry and our perpetual fountain was silent. We walked amid the ruins. The heavy smell of smoke hung in the air, and huge, charred matchstick trees surrounded us on all sides as far as we could see over our entire property.

After the cabin area, we explored the spring hoping to find something from our efforts intact. Though the steel filtration tank still stood behind it, all trace of the PVC pipe was gone. Even the heavy-duty 3,000-gallon polypropylene water storage tank was flattened like a pancake. Up farther at the springhead, we found the steel spring box to be completely intact. But that was it. As I prayed silently that the animals had somehow outrun the fire, Gary ahead of me suddenly whispered,

"Look!" And up ahead past the spring box stood a deer with her fawn, unhurt. She just stood looking back at us, unafraid and (like us) almost dazed. It occurred to me that she knew us, probably having seen us many times before on our cabin visits. (Later, as we drove out, we encountered two fully grown bears still within all the charred timber. The first ran directly in front of us across the road at top speed, the other a distance later was in the road ahead of us and ran down the hill. Both were unhurt. My prayers, at least in part seemed to be answered.)

Then we walked down from the cabin past Mountain Lion Rock to see the spring water gushing down the hillside, and literally spilling out crystal clear through the end of the culvert that protruded on the other side of the road. Now and then, I could hear a loud *snap* and then a *thud*. In the distance, the sound of a crashing tree reverberated in the stillness of the unreal atmosphere. It was as though we were in a catastrophic war zone. I told Gary that we still had our memories, even if the fire had taken this lovely place from us physically.

Mother Nature is so whimsical and indiscriminate and yet God is so merciful. In the midst of this, we really rejoiced and truly thanked God that our friends' cabins had been spared; Dan and Robin's, two others, and of course Bill's (who'd labored a lifetime there—lovingly in his spare time building an additional cabin and a state-of –the-art off-grid power system and communications network). So much multi-generational history was in all of them. The historic lookout we found out later was also saved.

Strangely, as we walked back up the hill to our truck to head back down the mountain, our Greta, who had surveyed and sniffed everything out in her own way, put the entire thing into perfect perspective. As Gary began taking photos with his phone for insurance purposes, Greta meandered over to the edge of what had been our lawn, where our heavy iron BBQ caldron remained relatively unscathed. She sniffed a bit and lay down close to her spot on a corner of the charred lawn that was still intact. Life had just handed her a lemon too, and she'd made the best of it.

Later, as we drove out, after our bear encounters, we encountered a fire crew and stopped. I am glad we did, because they were eyewitnesses to what had happened to our cabin. It gave us both some closure. The captain came over to the side of our truck and spoke with Gary through the window. Learning that we had been to our cabin site, he said that he was very familiar with it and was very sorry. He'd remembered our cabin from the scouting mission of the previous year, admitting with a smile that he'd looked into the windows and played a round of horseshoes there, wishing he had a cabin in the forest like ours. But then he shook his head and said somberly that there was no saving it this time. From below, where they helplessly watched the uncontrollable, raging fire, they witnessed firsthand our cabin burn. The flames, he said, must have shot up to four hundred feet high.

Even though we thought we had fire protection that could mitigate damage—having the land cleared, roads widened, water available, and hydrants on standby—it wasn't enough. A fire is awesome in its power. I am glad we got out in time. My husband fought these kinds of fires in his spare time for the then-named CDF, (California Division of Forestry, now called CALFIRE) many years earlier on his D7 CAT. He told me that a fire creates a perfect storm and brings a hurricane of wind with it. Often he fought them at night, seeing this type of havoc first hand, and experiencing more than one near-death experience.

▲ The cabin site wiped clean after Gary had heavy equipment in and cleaned it up as though it never was. All that remains was part of the log railing, which we left untouched.

(I've told him he's worn out at least a dozen guardian angels to date.)

But, all this said, DO NOT let this news deter you. Remember, chance always favors a prepared mind. I didn't tell you all this to change your mind about finding your cabin in the forest. I just want you to think ahead. Get that insurance policy up front, as we did. When we purchased the cabin, the first thing we did was contact our agent, Steve Mora, who owns Heritage Insurance, and is affiliated with Grange Insurance. He was in contact with us during the renovation process. We provided him with photos and also documentation of the property and its value. I cannot stress enough the importance of having photos on hand, both of the structures and the contents of your cabin. We do the same for our home's property. In addition, as luck would have it, Skyhorse Publishing in New York had accepted my book, and thankfully my editor wanted *lots* of photos. So, I painstakingly took in my photo album to CVS and sat at the print booth for about four hours scanning a couple hundred photos to two CDs. Little did I know those CDs would help pave the way for our insurance claim to be processed quickly and to our satisfaction. The claims adjuster who followed us up to the cabin a mere two to three weeks later told us how glad he was to have so much physical evidence, because when there is nothing left it is hard to picture what had been there. In effect, it made his report much more thorough. Our total insured amount was easily met, if not surpassed. And we had our first check for the structures within six to eight weeks of the fire. Checks for the contents soon followed. Amazing. Pictures do speak a thousand words. I can say it made a terribly painful experience much less painful for us.

In addition, Steve informed us that we could move a percentage of the insurance policy coverage for our home's contents coverage amount to cover the cabin contents, giving us compensation beyond the structures' insured amount. It was a godsend. You may also be able to transfer coverage in this way if, heaven forbid, the need arises. As part of a fire damage claim, our insurance even allowed for an additional amount of funds (a percentage of the total insured value) to be paid for the cleanup and debris removal. In fact, we just completed cleanup this spring.

And as for us and our future? We have definitely not ruled out another adventure. I learned when I was

▲ After the fire. The view shows where the cabin entrance used to be. The rainbow image only appeared after the photo was taken and I viewed the image. It was not visible when I took the photo of the cleaned-up site. We took that rainbow as an omen, meaning that everything was going to be okay.

young that when the horse throws you off, you have to get right up, dust yourself off and get back in the saddle.

Conclusion

When I asked Gary about his thoughts and advice to share with you about your own cabin dwelling, be it like Jill's year-round 24/7 self-sufficient lifestyle, our type cabin in the forest as a retreat, or something in between, he had this to offer: "Everyone has their own dream of the perfect off-grid cabin lifestyle to experience. Just be aware of this: it doesn't come without work, innovation, or maintenance and upkeep." But is it worth it? You've gleaned more than enough from this book to know the answer is a resounding *Yes*. So go for it!